PSYCHOANALYTIC ASPECTS OF ASSISTED
REPRODUCTIVE TECHNOLOGY

PSYCHOANALYTIC ASPECTS OF ASSISTED REPRODUCTIVE TECHNOLOGY

Edited by
Mali Mann

KARNAC

First published in 2014 by
Karnac Books Ltd
118 Finchley Road
London NW3 5HT

British Library Cataloguing in Publication Data

A C.I.P. for this book is available from the British Library

ISBN-13: 978-1-78049-196-7

Typeset by V Publishing Solutions Pvt Ltd., Chennai, India

Printed in Great Britain

www.karnacbooks.com

To the loving memory of my mother
Moloud Abadian, an educator
who inspired me how to relieve human pain and love knowledge

And my father
Amir Yaghoub Amirsoleimani, a humanitarian
who believed in human rights and equality

CONTENTS

ABOUT THE EDITOR AND CONTRIBUTORS

Diane Ehrensaft, PhD, is the director of mental health and founding member of the Child and Adolescent Center and a clinical psychologist in San Francisco Bay Area, in Oakland, California. Her research and writing focus on the areas of child development, gender, parenting, parent–child relationships, and psychological issues for families using assisted reproductive technology. She has published several books and articles in these areas, and lectures and makes media appearances nationally and internationally on these topics. She also serves on the Board of Gender Spectrum, a national organisation offering educational, training, and advocacy services to promote gender acceptance for youth of all diverse genders. She does parenting consultation, custody mediation, and co-parenting counselling in her practice. Dr Ehrensaft is a senior consultant, founding member, and board member of A Home Within, a national project focused on the emotional needs of children and young people in foster care, offering *pro bono* long-term psychotherapy to children in foster care.

Katherine MacVicar, MD, is a psychoanalyst and training and supervising analyst at the San Francisco Center for Psychoanalysis. Her main interest and area of study are the theoretical and clinical ideas of the

British Kleinians and their application to the analysis of primitive and psychotic states of mind. She has held the position of president of the San Francisco Center for Psychoanalysis and the chair of the education committee at the Center. She has been involved in psychoanalytic film discussion in the East Bay, California, for over two decades. She was a co-chair of a discussion group on neo-Kleinians taking place at the American Psychoanalytic Association for many years.

Andrea Mann, DO, MPhil, is a psychiatrist, bioethicist, and epidemiologist. She completed a master's degree in epidemiology at the University of Cambridge prior to attending medical school at Western University of Health Sciences. As a resident in psychiatry, she trained at the University of Chicago, where she completed a fellowship through the MacLean Center for Clinical Medical Ethics. She has several interests, which include the ethical and psychological impact of reproductive health; mental health in physically ill children; use of psychotropic medication in vulnerable populations; clinical decision-making; and psychodynamic psychotherapy. She has written several papers in peer-reviewed journals on these topics.

Mali Mann, MD, is on the faculty of the San Francisco Center for Psychoanalysis, where she serves as a training and supervising psychoanalyst. She is also a clinical professor, adjunct at the Department of Psychiatry and Behavioral Sciences, Stanford University, where she is a member of Pegasus Physicians writing group. She is a faculty member and supervisor at San Mateo county psychiatry residency programme. She currently serves as the co-chair for the North American Committee of Child and Adolescent Psychoanalysis. She teaches and supervises candidates at Palo Alto psychoanalytic psychotherapy training programme. She has authored several chapters and psychoanalytic papers, and has served on several local and national psychoanalytic committees. Her interests focus on identity formation, immigrant children and mothers, the dynamics of shame, aggression in clinical settings, and applied psychoanalysis in orphanages and the school system. In addition, she has a special interest in maternal development and immigrant motherhood, and holds membership of the American Society of Reproductive Medicine.

Monisha Nayar-Akhtar, PhD, is a training and supervising analyst at the Psychoanalytic Center of Philadelphia. She is an adult and child/adolescent psychoanalyst and trained at the Michigan Psychoanalytic Institute. She has a full-time practice in Ardmore, Pennsylvania. She has a special interest in the psychoanalytic study of trauma. She has edited a book on *Play and Playfulness*, and is interested in cultural variations in and the clinical implications of play and play therapy.

Terese Schulman, PhD, is a psychoanalyst and member of the American Psychoanalytic Society. She is a member of the San Francisco Center for Psychoanalysis. She has a special interest in women's development, motherhood, and assisted reproductive technology. She has written on psychological impediments to motherhood. Her private practice is in Oakland and Corte Madera, California.

Psychoanalytic impact of assisted reproductive technology

Mali Mann

The recent and rapid advances in reproductive technologies confront us with the need to understand their complex psychological impact on children who are born through these procedures and on their families. As a physician and psychoanalyst, I became aware of my patients' trouble accepting their infertility after drawn-out attempts to have their own children. Acceptance of their failure to conceive is more of a challenge for some patients than others, although often there may never be a final acceptance. This book developed over the course of thirty years, from my own clinical experience working with infertile women in psychotherapy and psychoanalysis. Many of these women struggled with various forms of assisted reproductive technology (ART).

Assisted reproductive technologies are methods for infertile couples to achieve pregnancy by artificial or partially artificial means. ART includes in-vitro fertilisation, intra-cytoplasmic sperm injection (ICSI), cryopreservation, and intra-uterine insemination (IUI). There has been a dearth of research on the psychological impact of these methods on the human psyche. This book is an attempt to highlight the crucial importance of integrative work on the part of psychotherapists and psychoanalysts with reproductive medical specialists. Clinical psychoanalytic and psychotherapeutic help plays an important role in making the use of modern reproductive technology more likely to lead to positive outcomes for everyone involved.

Undoubtedly, the discovery of infertility is fraught with feelings of loss, fear, shame, and grief for the individual and for the couple. The fear and unremitting dread can be overwhelming and lead to a feeling of shame for not being able to produce a biological child. When confronted with repeated failure to conceive, a couple may seek medical and in some cases psychological support. The decision to see a specialist is an affirmation of their infertility.

Infertility can be experienced as an overpowering sense of emptiness and anxiety. There may be a vacillation between hope and bleak despair. A cycle of excitement followed by despair and disappointment can repeat itself many times. Depression, guilt, and apprehension may take hold. The infertility can turn into a monthly assault on feelings of masculinity or femininity and can provoke a sense of identity crisis. The couples who fail to conceive may question their value as men and women, seeing themselves as "defective".

This book brings together my colleagues' as well as my own collective clinical experience working with patients touched by ART. The chapters cover a variety of topics related to the use of assisted reproductive technology and the role of unconscious transaction in analytic process. As analysts, we appreciate the value of in-depth understanding of a single case presentation. Shared themes from these cases are not meant to be generalisations, but could provide a starting point for future research on this topic. Further clinical research on the psychological impact of ART within families is needed.

Mali Mann authors the chapter entitled "Repetition compulsion and psychoanalytic understanding of repeated IVF trials and failures". She discusses two detailed case histories, which illustrate how infertility traumata were re-experienced compulsively. The unconscious self-induced traumatisation resulted from the compulsion to repeat an earlier repressed trauma. The denial of multiple and repeated failures illustrates a complex compilation of several unprocessed losses that the individuals have yet to finish mourning.

In addition, the lack of acceptance of a failure to conceive presented itself as a technical challenge offering an understanding of repeated past experiences in the context of the transference and countertransference paradigm. Each new IVF cycle followed the unprocessed mourning of a loss with persistence to repeat. The repeating of the past experiences over and over in a rather fast-paced use of ARTs shows the strong evidence for dynamic repetition compulsion phenomena. The denial of the failure to conceive can linger on, becoming a long process with unfinished mourning throughout the life cycle. The need for psychoanalytic thinking and understanding of psychological implications of the use of in-vitro fertilisation (IVF) and other similar procedures is emphasised in this chapter.

Diane Ehrensaft, in her chapter entitled "Family complexes and oedipal circles", provides a sophisticated review of Donald Winnicott's work, extrapolating that there is no baby without a mother. In building a family using ART, there is no baby without all the people who intend to have the baby, including all who contribute to the conception or gestation of that baby (that is, gamete donor or surrogate carrier). That grouping coalesces into the "family complex", a relational system that every child born into such a family must negotiate as he or she takes on three unique developmental tasks: 1) self-concept/individuality: am I different?; 2) bonding and attachment: who do I belong to?; and 3) identity formation: who am I? This chapter explores the complicated parent–child relationships, both conscious and unconscious, when a baby is conceived or gestated with the assistance of an outside party, be it sperm donor, egg donor, surrogate, gestational carrier, or some combination thereof, referred to in the chapter as "birth others". The complexity of these interpersonal and intrapersonal dynamics is then discussed in the context of an expanded traditional oedipal triangle. A new oedipal circle is described. Children must negotiate each of the developmental tasks listed above as they incorporate their "birth other" origins into their internal object world. The discussion is based on extensive clinical data about children, parents, parent–child relations, and families in relationship to their donors, surrogates, or gestational carriers. Ehrensaft describes the family complex in the context of modern-day family formation and offers a possible revision of the classical oedipal construct.

Terese Schulman presents two cases in a chapter entitled "Psychoanalytic treatment of anxiety related to motherhood and the use of ART". Schulman notes that some women delay making the decision to have children because of their unconscious fears. She describes the growing trend of professional women in their late thirties and early forties presenting to analytic treatment to explore their ambivalence about motherhood. While their fertility nears an end, sexual difficulties coincide with ambivalence towards achieving motherhood. These women seek psychotherapy because they are unable to find meaningful, lasting loving relationships. They struggle with finding a satisfying sexual relationship and forming a committed partnership that would provide a safe environment in which to consider motherhood. Their problematic identification (often dis-identification) with their mothers is found to be related to their difficulties in pursuing an available partner and having a satisfying sexual relationship that might lead to parenthood.

Schulman describes her psychoanalytic therapies with her two cases. She works with their anxieties and the conflicts that caused them to delay motherhood, and eventually to require ART to achieve a pregnancy. The less intense but re-emerging anxieties require additional work in order for these women to move forward into motherhood.

Mali Mann and Andrea Mann describe three cases in psychodynamic psychotherapy illustrating the complex psychological ramifications of ART. The cases are compelling examples of identification and dis-identification with primary maternal objects, presenting conflict in the formation of parental identity. The themes of secrecy and sense of shame are the underlying struggles for these individuals who go through infertility medical work-up and use ART. During those procedures, the levels of fear, anxiety, and the resurgence of old conflicts escalate to an unbearable level. This fresh perspective into the world of egg and sperm donors offers an important insight into today's parenting identity formation. Infertility impacts on one's self-identity as a mother or father, and these individuals have to deal with unexpected emotions, which depend on their personality styles, the maturity of their defence mechanisms, and external support systems.

Monisha Nayar-Akhtar, in "Infertility, trauma and assisted reproductive technology", explores how childhood trauma and the decision to use ART arise in two psychoanalytical cases. These two women had histories of conceiving children using ART and sought treatment for depression, anxiety, and other psychological problems much later in their lives. During the course of treatment, the patients' anxieties, fears, and fantasies of ART are further elaborated and examined. The issues surrounding such choices are profound and are evaluated in the context of the psychoanalytic literature.

Katherine MacVicar, in the last chapter of the book, discusses a contemporary film entitled *The Kids Are All Right*. MacVicar describes the marital life of a lesbian couple raising two children who were conceived through the help of an anonymous sperm donor and the use of ART. Issues unique to children conceived through ART include the absent parent, curiosity about how and why they were "made", and parental sexuality. These issues have a somewhat different valence because of ART, and in this case because the parents are homosexual.

The film is also about adolescent development and the relational challenges, shifting loyalties, peer group tensions, superego modifications, and identity formations that accompany this stage. There are fluctuations in these adolescents' level of trust when they face their biological father. The film depicts the dynamics of their trust–betrayal–conflict and identity–confusion–consolidation almost to the level of good-enough optimal state given the turbulent setting of their development and home environment.

My purpose in this introduction is to provide the reader with a glimpse of the issues that arise through analytical work as individuals engage in ART to achieve their personal family goals. Analysts are able to help their patients become aware of their inner turmoil while they experience traumatic reproductive procedures. Understanding the mental landscape of individuals struggling with infertility will help practitioners to develop the empathy required to ease emotional unrest. Helping individuals develop introspection into their internal worlds and to become aware of unconscious conflicts that are hard to bear are important therapeutic goals. Offering opportunities to help our patients will ease their emotional burdens at such a challenging and agonising time. Additionally, working in collaboration with medical reproductive specialists can help improve the emotional outcomes for all parties involved.

PART I

CLINICAL PERSPECTIVES

CHAPTER ONE

Psychoanalytic understanding of repeated in-vitro fertilisation trials, failures, and repetition compulsion

Mali Mann

Recent advances in reproductive technology and the increased use of techniques based upon it have created a need for psychoanalytic thinking and understanding of the psychological implications of in-vitro fertilisation (IVF) and other similar procedures. The recent and rapid advances in medical technologies confront us with the mandate to understand their complex impact on parents and their children.

As a physician and psychoanalyst, I became aware of my patients' trouble accepting their infertility after drawn-out, repeated attempts to have their own children. The acceptance of their failure in conceiving is more of a challenge for some patients than others, although sometimes there can never be a final acceptance. The denial of their failure as a couple to conceive can become a long process with unfinished mourning throughout their life cycle.

The two cases in this chapter in particular illustrate how infertility traumata were re-experienced. The unconscious self-induced traumatisation resulted from the compulsion to repeat an earlier repressed trauma.

Freud inferred the existence of motivation beyond the pleasure principle. In 1919, he postulated "the principle of repetition compulsion of the unconscious mind, based upon instinctual activity and probably inherent in the very nature of the instincts—a principle powerful enough to overrule the pleasure-principle". Building on his 1914 article "Remembering, Repeating and Working-Through", Freud highlighted how the "patient cannot remember the whole of what is repressed in him, and is obliged to *repeat* the repressed material as a contemporary experience instead of … *remembering* it as something belonging to the past: a compulsion to repeat".

Those individuals who can better accept their infertility without significant psychological complication resort to other methods of becoming parents to fulfil their life-long expectation. Some may take an alternative step and adopt someone else's child. Some infertile individuals whose infertility is related to their advanced age use alternative procedures such as in-vitro fertilisation (IVF). In today's world, many women want to establish themselves in their careers and choose to postpone reproductive goals until later. When they face reproductive failure, they become extremely anxious, especially when the biological clock is ticking away faster and faster. The narcissistic injury is deep and debases their belief system about self-representation and their body image. Women are affected profoundly by fertility failure. They carry with them the identification linkage with their primary pre-oedipal maternal object, wanting to become a parent. We see clinically girls who play mother roles in fantasy. Once a woman's pregnancy wishes are frustrated, the denial of an infertile self-image could potentially lead to crisis.

The way in which these women react to the trauma of their infertility will determine a number of factors, including how they choose to use a donor egg, donor sperm, or surrogate mother. The character of their traumatic experience also influences the process of deciding who will donate their egg, their sperm, or their womb.

Though the reasoning varies among theories, experts agree that the ability to become a mother is essential to believing that one is viable as a woman. Freud (1940a) made passing reference to the subject of human reproduction and pregnancy. The primacy of sexuality in human life for Freud is reflected in his belief that the wish for a child in the woman represents the symbolic substitution for the missing penis; a wish for reparation and completion.

Helene Deutsch (1945) questioned the reparative function of the woman's procreative life. She made it clear that the woman's urge to become pregnant and bear a child represents the essentially feminine quality of receptiveness, a bio-physiological concept, the bedrock of femininity.

Benedek (1952), and Bibring and colleagues (1961), pioneers in the study of women's reproductive drive, saw pregnancy as a developmental crisis, and subsequent writers seem to accept this view (Lester & Notman, 1988).

In severely traumatised women, the wish to be pregnant is not necessarily connected to the wish for a child, as seen by Pines (1982). Pregnancy, instead, is simply seen as an effort to repair the narcissistic injury of early life.

Pines (1982) elaborated on the mother–daughter relationship as the locus of psychic conflict in women who abort habitually. Pre-oedipal dynamics were discussed and identified by Lester and Notman (1986, 1988) as causing anxieties during the early stages of pregnancy.

In her paper "Infertility in the Age of Technology" (1999), Zallusky highlighted the effect of infertility on the analytic process. She elaborates on the permeability of the boundaries between analyst and patient, and between fantasy and action, in psychoanalytic work with women who are infertile and resort to assisted reproductive technology (ART).

The immense stress of infertility can trigger regressions to earlier stages of psychological development. Intense feelings of envy and shame felt currently conflict with their roots in childhood, bringing about a disturbance to the person's sense of self-identity. As Freud stated, the ego "is first and foremost a body ego" (1923b, p. 27). The earliest way in which we know ourselves is through our body.

Kite (2009) emphasised the importance of keeping the emotional reality of the patient in view in a panel on "Current Perspectives on Infertility", in which the motivations for childbearing were discussed in relation to ART.

The entry of a third person—the doctor—into the sexual relationship, as if into the primal scene, is another theme in some of the literature. Also in the context of surrogate mothers and/or sperm donation, Ehrensaft (2008) described the feelings and fantasies of parents in relation to having another, outside party involved in conception. She described a stirring up of fantasies of a *ménage à trois*. She observed that the egg donation or the surrogate could stir up fantasies of the other.

Thinking of the sperm as *sperm* may be defensive against thinking of the sperm as coming from another whole person. Ehrensaft also pointed out the importance of telling children about their origins.

Coming to terms with infertility or mourning can manifest as a problem not only for women, but also for men and for the entity of the couple.

In-vitro fertilisation

In-vitro fertilisation means "fertilisation under glass", that is, in a test tube. IVF is a technique for removing eggs from a woman, fertilising them outside her body, and placing the fertilised egg, or embryo, directly into the uterus. All IVF procedures have four steps: ovarian stimulation, egg retrieval, fertilisation, and embryo transfer.

Overcoming infertility was unimaginable just a generation or two ago. Since then, scientists have devised a way to remove the sperm and eggs and combine them. Eggs are fertilised, then frozen for future use; sperm strength can be boosted; and even women who lack ovaries may find themselves pregnant. These procedures arouse much curiosity among the general public and within the broad community of infertility and mental health experts.

The first "test-tube baby" was born in 1978. Louise Brown was the first child to be conceived by in-vitro fertilisation and was delivered after a full-term pregnancy. In the few years since, IVF has become an important element in the vocabulary of infertility. It has become the cutting edge of modern reproductive treatment and research.

In-vitro fertilisation requires intact fecundity, normal production of ova. Today, a number of women in their mid- to late thirties and early forties, in spite of their intense desire to conceive, remain infertile. Fecundity is intact in many of these subjects, and advances in reproductive technology make it possible to overcome infertility in some of these cases. New ground continues to be broken as research continues.

Regardless of the cause of infertility, the treatment that leads to the highest pregnancy rate per cycle is in-vitro fertilisation. Since its inception in 1978, there has been a remarkable increase in the numbers of IVF cycles worldwide (Nachtigall & Mehren, 1991). Approximately one in fifty births in Sweden, one in sixty births in Australia, and one in eighty to a hundred births in the United States now result from IVF. In 2003, more than 100,000 IVF cycles were reported from 399 clinics in the United States, resulting in the birth of more than 48,000 babies. IVF is now the treatment that leads to the highest pregnancy rate per cycle (Van Voorhis, 2007).

Egg donation was introduced in the 1980s, increasing the possibility of pregnancy and childbearing for many women. Many of the women receiving these donations were older and had delayed childbearing for reasons such as establishing careers, personal conflict, and ambivalent feelings about becoming mothers. These women, and also those who had had illnesses the treatment of which affected their fertility, were then able to have children. Still, egg donation brought up a great deal of controversy. In addition to the ethical dilemma, egg donation presents issues such as parental identity confusion and compromised sense of social group belongingness. I have encountered many clinical examples of this, but expounding upon them would be beyond the scope of this chapter.

The use of surrogates—women who carry a pregnancy for another individual or couple—generates further possibilities for women unable to conceive. The baby can have the genetic identity of the couple—that is, the ovum can be obtained from the woman in the couple and be fertilised by the man's sperm and then implanted in the woman who has agreed to be the surrogate—or the surrogate can supply the ovum and the sperm can be the husband's or come from a donor. This has made having a genetically related baby possible for gay couples, as well as for women who for some reason, such as repeated pregnancy loss, cannot carry a baby to term but have viable ova. It is possible to freeze sperm, eggs, or embryos for later use.

Implanting more than one embryo increases the likelihood of having a viable pregnancy. It also increases the likelihood of multiple births, which carry greater risks. The decision to reduce one or more embryos to prevent multiple implantations is a difficult one.

In this chapter, I do not focus on the traumatic effect of infertility. Instead, I discuss the use of multiple IVF trials despite repeated failures. One of the cases I discuss, for example, presents a serious narcissistic injury and disappointment at the discovery of infertility, which in turn affected the decision to use and the process of assisted reproductive technology. The delay in decision-making created medical risks during this woman's pregnancies. She insisted on going through a second pregnancy using her own uterus to carry a foetus that came from the union of her husband's sperm and an egg donor, her niece.

Unexplained infertility

No matter how sophisticated the technique used to combat infertility, there are cases in which a woman remains infertile. Some causes of infertility remain beyond our understanding, even in these days of enlightened biological technology and modern-day high-tech reproductive procedures. These as-yet unsolved mysteries are very frustrating to those trying to understand why some people can conceive and others cannot.

Unexplained infertility is a "diagnosis of exclusion". This means that all other known diagnoses must be eliminated before the infertility can fairly be called "unexplained". Making claims about the causality of infertility and the concept of psychogenic infertility is not a useful argument for us as psychoanalysts. Conscious and unconscious hostility towards a defective male sibling (Allison, 1997), and a woman's unconscious repudiated femininity or motherhood, can be important dynamics. However, there are couples who are able to conceive naturally in spite of similar dynamics. We need to be careful not to confuse the correlational data with causality.

In recent years, infertility treatment has undergone a genuine revolution, which has raised the possibilities for empirical treatment. Today's infertility treatment is referred to as "assisted reproductive technology"; most simply stated, ART represents the joining of a hormonal therapy with a form of artificial insemination. ART is most commonly represented by intra-uterine insemination (IUI), IVF, and IVF's variations.

Case one: Jean

Jean, a married forty-eight-year-old woman, came to see me for analysis after a hiatus in her psychotherapy. During her previous years of treatment with me when she was in her early forties, she saw me twice a week. She did not know why she could not conceive. She decided to wait and try natural methods to get pregnant. She made many attempts over a long period of time to conceive, without any success.

Jean's professional life was a trying and challenging one and kept her very occupied to the point that she lost track of passing years. She did take pride in her work and wanted to appear to her colleagues as "perfect" and "flawless".

Jean's inability to conceive was very difficult for her to accept, since she thought nothing was physically wrong with her. Male factors for infertility were ruled out. It meant to her that she was defective. Jean's husband, who was in a similar professional field, was very supportive of her; and he was willing to adopt or even be childless if Jean chose not to have any children.

Jean was shame-ridden about being defective and not being able to have children as her mother did. She felt intense envy towards her mother and especially her sister, who was five years her senior and had one son. Her envy of pregnant women was very intense, making her angry when she encountered pregnant women.

Jean came from a deprived background both emotionally and financially. She had memories of not having food and going hungry to school. She was not sure if she was conceived out of wedlock. She believed her sister was so conceived, and in her fantasy she thought her father never married her mother.

Jean's brother was born when she was eight years old. She remembers her parents were overjoyed because they finally had a son after so many years. Jean devalued her mother for her emotional detachment, but would also show guilty feelings for her rage towards her mother.

In her day-to-day interactions, Jean lacked emotional responsiveness. She tried hard to be friendly with her colleagues, as long as they praised her at work. She had many superficial friendships, but she could not go beyond the surface level in relationships.

At the beginning of our work, this patient had immediate realistic concerns about dying before she could fulfil her dream of becoming a mother. Her resistance to becoming fully involved in the transference was expressed in the form of overvaluing her job, dealing with life and death issues, and considering her analysis "just talking", a process in which "not much important action was happening".

Jean related that no matter how much insight she would gain through our work, she still needed to take action by hurrying to have children from her own eggs before it was too late. She wanted her gynaecologist to give her strong fertility medication like Lupron and other infertility medications to make her fertile. She went through multiple IVF procedures during this period. Each time they harvested her eggs, she would come in and boast about how many of *her own* eggs they were able to harvest. She turned a blind eye to the factual comments that several experts made to her about her age factor, which made her eggs unsuitable for IVF. She knew that the probability of getting a viable embryo using her ovum was very low. She vehemently defended her decision and said, "I just do not want to borrow another woman's eggs".

"Borrowing" another woman's eggs would mean that Jean was inferior to egg donors. After her husband suggested that perhaps they could consider an anonymous donor, though, she assented. Yet she waffled. If she could only find an anonymous donor from another country, perhaps she would follow through. In the end, Jean turned away from making the decision.

At this stage of our work, she was obsessed with going through many cycles of IVF without showing much interest in exploring the meaning of her desperate actions. Only after many failures in conceiving did Jean begin to wonder why she could not get pregnant. She thought she was either being punished or she was just flawed. Her almost total absence of fantasy material towards me gradually gave way to being intensively curious about my personal life after she inadvertently learned that I had a daughter. Having found out through a friend who attended a fundraising event where I was participating with my daughter, Jean imagined that I must be an attentive mother myself and not like her own mother who was aloof and detached. She would use technical terms to show me that she was psychologically minded and a well-read, intellectual woman. However, she would mispronounce or misuse words and quickly apologise to me for not having used the word accurately.

Jean would come to her sessions punctually, and she would get anxious when I took a break for a holiday or professional travel. She worried that I would never come back and that some disaster would separate us forever.

Gradually, the intense fear of her rage and somatic complaints gave way to uncovering the meaning of her dread over anything emotionally valuable in her life. She had intense envy of me as her analyst, and in fantasy wanted to exchange my rich and fulfilling life as a mother for her own barren existence.

In one of our sessions, after complaining that she had spent so many years of life in analysis without much change in her grief over being flawed (she still believed she was flawed), she agreed with my comment that I, too, must have failed her not to have given her the wisdom of my knowledge and experience; like her mother, I, too, have given birth to a barren analytic child who was infertile. She acknowledged that although she agreed with much of what I said, she still had not given up on going through yet another IVF trial at her age. She was sure

I could be not happy with her inability to conceive and that I would interpret it as if we both had failed.

Jean's conflict around unconscious envy of me emerged as an expression of hatred and distrust of her mother. Her sense of competitiveness also emerged as she wished to have a sense of triumph instead of missed opportunities. Her denial of reality regarding her advanced age for a successful IVF outcome continued to take the centre stage of our analytic work.

Jean continued to seek the creation of a baby from her own eggs fertilised by her husband's sperm. After seven trials without any success, she regretted putting herself through such vigorous procedures for a woman her age. She became more interested in the meaning of her loss. Finally, she had to face it and go through the grief stage. She realised that she could no longer hold on to her dream.

At the end, Jean realised that she could neither have a genetically related child, nor could she accept another woman's egg. After all, she could not picture herself as a nurturing mother, and she concluded that it may be for the best not to become a mother. She could not be like her own fertile mother and had to accept the reality of growing old. Finally, she was able to face her ambivalence. Jean could learn to be more nurturing to the vulnerable part of herself.

At this point, the memory of her brother's birth came up and her rivalry with him became a central theme in our work. The following is an example of how Jean characterised her envy:

PATIENT: I have all these mean thoughts and I feel really bad.
ANALYST: Carrying the mean thoughts makes you feel guilt.
PATIENT: It is very very harmful to be occupied with them.
ANALYST: In our last hour, you mentioned how hard it was to deal with jealousy at your brother's birth.
PATIENT: Yes, Mom was mad at me for being jealous of my brother. I am never good enough. Other people have talents and value, not me. There is this other part of me that is irrational and unkind. There was always a feeling about my chance of getting pregnant with IVFs. How many attempts I made to give birth was like pushing a pickle through a straw. How many mean thoughts I would have! I am trying to make sense of these feelings. I am flawed, but I want to be saintly and have power to make these women lose their babies or relinquish

them when they are born. I have those mean, evil thoughts.
I am torn again all the time.

It ran through my mind that if i had special power, the
technology would have worked for me. I would have gotten
pregnant by now. Technology is amazing and works for
others, but not me. There is a zinger in that. I did not want
to have a flawed child, so maybe it was for the best that I did
not get pregnant.

After many years of attempts, Jean was in a place to make a decision to
adopt a one-year-old girl from China. This was a reasonable compromise for her after so many years of struggling with her desire to have
her own biological child. Our analytical work had helped her to work
through her early mother–daughter and oedipal conflicts.

Case two: Fran

Fran was a forty-eight-year-old lawyer who came to see me because of
depressive symptoms and romantic disinterest in her husband. She was
hurt and angry because her husband became emotionally involved with
a woman at his work. She thought her husband had become detached
because she was putting all of her effort into using reproductive technology to get pregnant.

Before her current marriage, she had been briefly married to a man
who was very critical of her weight even though she was a woman of
normal weight. They divorced after one year.

She remarried at age forty after four years of a long-distance relationship with the man who became her husband. Her husband is an
architect whom she met while she attended law school. Their sexual
attraction and their individual interest in sexual activity diminished
over time until this became non-existent.

Fran was interested in having children and tried without success to
get pregnant in the earlier years of her marriage. She and her husband
went through a reproductive/fertility work-up and did intra-uterine
insemination without success. In the same year, it was discovered
that her uterus had three large myoma (non-cancerous tumours).
She underwent a myomectomy and then tried to get pregnant naturally. After many months without success, she went through six IVF
procedures.

Each time, Fran repeated the cycle of overstimulation of the ovaries, harvesting the eggs, in-vitro fertilisation, and freezing of the viable embryos. She would become very hopeful and when the transfer failed, she would come to her sessions crying in silence and going through another cycle of unfinished grief work. Fran then quickly bounced back and wanted to try IVF again. Her denial about the loss of her youth, wanting to remain a young, fertile woman forever, was unshakable, and her sense of omnipotence governed her fantasy.

Fran came from a family of eight children. Her father was a professor and her mother a nurse. After the first three children became school age, her mother decided to have a second set of five children. Fran is the eldest of the second set.

Fran's father was overcritical and was frequently away travelling. Her mother was nurturing to the younger children, but the older ones were neglected. Fran had to take care of her younger siblings and did not have much private time for herself. She grew angrier each time her mother got pregnant.

Her mother's fertility was the topic of Fran's conversations with her friends and in her therapy. Fran's conflict about motherhood was significant during the early years of her marriage. There were psychological as well as physical factors in her infertility that interfered with her becoming pregnant. She dis-identified with her mother, who was "fruitful and multiplied".

As time progressed, Fran became aware of time's passage and questioned her childlessness. She became anxious and rushed to remedy her infertility by choosing to become a mother despite her inability to conceive naturally. Fran was influenced by unconscious psychological factors. Her unconscious repudiation of her femininity played an important role in her difficulty conceiving.

During her psychoanalytic treatment, Fran's developmental achievement of greater autonomy helped her "own" her femininity more fully. This enabled her to see herself more as a mature woman who needed to embark on the motherhood phase of her life despite her advanced years.

Fran and her husband tried to get pregnant for over ten years. She was almost fifty when she went through her first IVF. Her doctor said the chance of success was very slim, but she wanted to go through with it anyway. When it failed, she became depressed and had to deal with the loss of a dream to have a child with her own egg. She was struggling with her own sense of omnipotence—with issues of creating life—in an ambivalent way, destroying life via denial of the reality of her advanced age. Through our analytic work, she gradually became aware of her intense repetition compulsion, accepting the reality of her ageing ova and ushering her body into the menopause phase of life.

With reluctance, Fran considered going through a search for an egg donor. She decided to ask her niece to become her donor. Her niece was a young woman, in her early twenties. Her niece agreed to go through the procedure for Fran with Fran's husband's sperm.

The IVF was successful and the healthy foetus was implanted in Fran's uterus. The clinic kept three more embryos for possible future pregnancies. Fran's pregnancy was normal and her delivery uneventful.

When her baby girl was born, Fran brought her to show me in my office. The girl had faint resemblance to her mother, and Fran admitted that she looked like her niece more than her. She was thankful that her daughter was physically healthy.

This case shows a happy ending in certain respects, and yet, there are many unanswered questions about Fran's family dynamics. What will happen when the child asks where she came from? When the little girl became a school-aged child, Fran was not ready to disclose the reality of her origins. She is working in treatment to understand the underlying meaning of her decision to keep this secret despite the fact that the rest of her family knows the child's origins.

Discussion

The two cases I described have a few psychological factors in common. Both women started rather late in their reproductive years to get pregnant. Their denials of their advanced age factor motivated both women to resort to repeated IVF trials without success. Both women had trouble accepting their infertility and insisted on having their own biological children.

Jean felt deficient and deprived. She felt it was her right to have a baby. She was envious of her mother, sister, and sister–in–law's abilities to have their own children, and she wondered why not her.

Jean was told her eggs may be defective, and her doctor advised her to use an egg donor. She was in despair and felt envious of her mother who did not have to go through a fertility work-up. Jean attributed her difficulty conceiving to her mother's belief that she could not carry a baby because of her delicate body frame. After all, her mother's prophecy must have come true. At last, Jean faced her infertility while she was going through her analytical work with me.

With Fran, once her pregnancy wishes were frustrated, the denial of her infertile self-image pushed her to a potential crisis level. Her repetition compulsion is related to her unconscious envy of her mother who was "fruitful and multiplied", having eight children, unlike her. After multiple trials, Fran accepted that the only way she could become pregnant was through a donor egg. She has not fully thought through the pros and cons of selecting a family member as her egg donor.

Both patients' narcissistic injuries were deep, and this debased their belief systems about their self-representations and their body images. They carry with them the identificatory linkage with their primary pre-oedipal maternal object, wanting to become parents. As we see clinically, girls play mother roles in fantasy. In reality, once their wishes are unfulfilled, the desire to get a different result than the one they face reaches a critical level. These conflicts propel them to try repeatedly to master the traumatic impact of their infertility.

Both women suffered from the trauma of having to go through reproductive technology. Jean took an alternative step and adopted a child, while Fran got pregnant with a donor egg.

Freud introduced the concept of repetition compulsion in "Remembering, Repeating and Working-Through" (1914g) and *Beyond the Pleasure Principle* (1920g). These essays marked a major turning point in Freud's theoretical approach. Previously, he had attributed most human behaviour to the sexual instinct (libido). He went "beyond" the simple pleasure principle, developing his theory of drives with the addition of the death drive (referred to as "Thanatos").

Freud examined the relationship between repetition compulsion and the pleasure principle. Although compulsive behaviours evidently satisfied some sort of drive, they were a source of direct un-pleasure. Somehow, "no lesson has been learnt from the old experience of these activities having led only to un-pleasure. In spite of that, they are repeated, under pressure of a compulsion." Freud concluded that the human psyche includes a compulsion to repeat that is independent of the pleasure principle.

In my clinical experiences working with a small group of women who have tried using IVF multiple times without any success, I saw clear evidence that unconsciously they resort to repeating a self-induced traumatic event. A compulsion to repeat was evident in my analytical work with women who went through multiple IVFs without a successful outcome.

One of the important factors in Jean's case—repeating the use of procedure—illustrated her attempt to repair her early childhood neglect and abandonment. What is particular in Jean's case is her nonchalant attitude about the doctor's repeated warnings against using her aged eggs. Her denial was persistent, yet through our work she could finally face the reality of her infertility.

Jean's fertility process required her to be away from her analysis for a prolonged period. Though, on one level, this was a matter of time, on another it was psychological; the reason she needed to be away was as a defence against intimacy with her analyst. One might think of her transference as a particular form of unconscious communication as appears in the projective identification process. She was abandoning me to fulfil her very important procreative goal—leaving a pre-oedipal mother.

Fran's case showed her significant conflict throughout her marriage. Aside from the physical factors that prolonged her attempts to get pregnant, she also had unconsciously dis-identified with her mother for fear of repeating her mother's fruitfulness in procreation.

Freud's repetition compulsion concept applies to these two cases in which the clinical phenomenon manifests with repetitive quality. However, analysis helped these two patients immensely with their aggressive conflicts as well as with the uncovering of their past trauma.

Freud cited four empirical observations as the basis for his theories and speculations: first, dreams occur in the traumatic neuroses in which patients repeat a traumatic situation; second, there is a tendency on patients' part to repeat painful experiences from the past during their analyses; third, the fate neuroses were an important notion; and fourth, certain types of children's play supports the concept of repetition.

In Moore and Fine's *Psychoanalytic Terms and Concepts* (1990), the meaning of the term "repetition compulsion" was extended to include drives for mastery as well as other adaptational and maturational processes. In Freud's speculations in *Beyond the Pleasure Principle* (1920g), the repetition compulsion is presented as an explanatory concept, inextricably tied to the death instinct. It functions as a regulatory principle, primitive in its origin and mechanisms, biologically based, and capable of overriding the pleasure/un-pleasure principle. Kubie (1939) stated that analysts after Freud have offered such diverse interpretations of the concept "as to render it almost meaningless" (p. 390).

Some contemporary authors believe that Freud's early concept of repetition compulsion is non-dynamic, negativistic, and fatalistic (Inderbitzin & Levy, 1998). There are many references to the repetition compulsion in psychoanalytic and psychiatric literature; I will list a selection that refers to the origin of the concept of compulsion to repeat and where it belongs in psychic structure.

Inderbitzin and Levy (1998) believe that one has to pay close attention to a more meaningful dynamic formulation, which includes a consideration of the intense frustration and ensuing aggression that trauma generates, and the opportunities for aggression provided by "re-experiencing trauma". Trauma appears to take on an instinct-like role that really belongs to the aggression created by the trauma. The re-experiences of trauma contain hidden aggressive aims and gratifications (often based on identification with the aggressor), including punishment of perpetrators by inducing guilt, demand for reparation, expression of entitlement, exploitation of others, magical "control" of helplessness, and purposeful self-defeat (self-directed aggression).

A woman's failure to conceive may be related to the traumatic and unsatisfactory relationship to her mother. The re-experience of trauma by repeated use of assisted reproductive technology such as IVF contains masked aggression, which is turned against self or others. The aggression may take the form of a demand for reparation and a magical solution to age-induced infertility. These two clinical illustrations show how infertility traumata were re-experienced as a new version of an earlier trauma with self-induced traumatisation through a compulsion to repeat.

References

Allison, G. H. (1997). Motherhood, motherliness, and psychogenic infertility. *Psychoanalytic Quarterly, 66*: 1–17.

Benedek, T. (1952). *Psychosocial Functions in Women*. New York: Ronald Press.

Bibring, G. L., Dwyer, T. F., Huntington, D. S., & Valenstein, A. F. (1961). A study of psychological process in pregnancy and of the earliest mother and child relationship. *Psychoanalytic Study of the Child, 16*: 9–72.

Deutsch, H. (1945). *The Psychology of Women*, Vol. II. New York: Grune and Stratton.

Ehrensaft, D. (2008). When baby makes three or four or more. *Psychanalytic Study of the Child, 63*: 3–23.

Freud, S. (1914g). "Remembering, Repeating and Working-Through" (Further Recommendations on the Technique of Psycho-Analysis II). *S. E., 12*. London: Hogarth.

Freud, S. (1920g). *Beyond the Pleasure Principle. S. E., 18*. London: Hogarth.

Freud, S. (1923b). *The Ego and the Id. S. E., 19*: 12–66. London: Hogarth.

Freud, S. (1926d). *Inhibitions, Symptoms and Anxiety. S. E., 20*. London: Hogarth.

Freud, S. (1940a). *An Outline of Psychoanalysis. S. E., 23*. London: Hogarth.

Inderbitzin, L. B., & Levy, S. (1998). Repetition compulsion revisited: implication for technique. *Psychoanalytic Quarterly, 67*: 32–53.

Kubie, L. S. (1939). A critical analysis of the concept of a repetition compulsion. *International Journal of Psycho-Analysis, 20*: 390–402.

Lester, E. P., & Notman, M. (1986). Pregnancy, developmental crisis and object relations: psychoanalytic considerations. *International Journal of Psychoanalysis, 62*: 357–366.

Nachtigall, R., & Mehren, E. (1991). *Overcoming Infertility: A Practical Strategy for Navigating the Emotional, Medical, and Financial Minefields of Trying to Have a Baby*. New York: Doubleday.

Notman, M., & Lester, E. P. (1988). Pregnancy: theoretical considerations. *Psychoanalytic Inquiry, 8*: 139–160.

Pines, D. (1982). Relevance of early development to pregnancy and abortion. *International Journal of Psychoanalysis, 61*: 311–318.

Van Voorhis, B. J. (2007). In vitro fertilization. *New England Journal of Medicine, 356*: 379–386.

Zallusky, S. (1999). Infertility in the age of technology. *Journal of the American Psychoanalytic Association, 48*: 1541–1562.

CHAPTER TWO

Family complexes and oedipal circles: mothers, fathers, babies, donors, and surrogates

Diane Ehrensaft

Introduction

We are now in a fertile new world in which men and women come together in a variety of combinations of gender, genetics, gamete dona-tion, and gestational carriers to make a baby. As these adults collabo-rate to give birth to a baby, they create a heretofore unheard of family complex: the matrix of all the individuals involved in the conception, gestation, or parenting of the intended child, along with that child and all the other offspring. This expansive family complex ushers in another new phenomenon. No longer will there be mummy, daddy, and baby makes three, a threesome that will later create an oedipal triangle. By the time baby comes around, up to six people may be involved in the conception and gestation of that baby—two social parents, an egg donor, a sperm donor, one gestational carrier, and a baby. This does not a triangle make. Rather, both the child and the other members of the family complex will find the triangle stretched to a circle as they negotiate the myriad of combinations of relationships involving all the players in the procreation process. Albeit they will discover triangles, squares, pentagons, even hexagons of relational connections within

19

that circle, depending on the number of participants in the assisted reproductive technology family complex and the child's knowledge of their existence. The question I am posing: What are the family dynamics and developmental implications for the child who must negotiate these complicated geometrics, as early as the third year of life?

My focus is on babies conceived or gestated with the aid of an outside party, be it sperm donor, egg donor, surrogate, or gestational carrier. Through a perhaps unconsciously intended typographical error while taking notes for my book *Mommies, Daddies, Donors, Surrogates*, I came upon an assignation for all of these outside parties as I omitted the "m" in "birth mother" and thereby invented "birth other": an individual involved in the birth process but an other rather than a parent to the child (Ehrensaft, 2005). So I will be using the term "birth other" to refer to donors, surrogates, or gestational carriers, and the term "birth other family" to refer to parents who create a family with the help of one or more of those outside parties.

Rethinking babies and their parents

... [W]e need to be ever watchful of the cultural lens from which we construct our theories of development and never take them as God's scientific word. (Ehrensaft, 2008a, p. 353)

I wrote this statement in an article critiquing the orthodox psychoanalytic concept of the oedipal stage but want to expand its scope to the more generalised task before us: altering our psychological theories of psychosocial and psychosexual development to fit the realities of twenty-first-century birth other families rather than try to contort these families to fit the assumptions of those nineteenth- and twentieth-century theories.

Even though the first sperm donor child came into the world as long ago as the 1880s,[1] our psychoanalytic forebears could hardly imagine a baby conceived without sexual intercourse or a baby gestated in a womb other than the genetic mother's. Sigmund Freud developed the construct of the Oedipus complex: the fantasy of incest with the opposite-sex parent combined with envy and rage towards the same-sex parent. Melanie Klein wrote of the precursor to the oedipal stage, the combined parental figure, which is the baby's phantasy that the parents, or more precisely their sexual organs, are locked together in permanent intercourse. Anna Freud warned that the lack of a father could lead to dangerous oedipal victory for a young boy:

> Where the father is absent owing to divorce, desertion, death, there is the lack of a restraining oedipal rival, a circumstance which intensifies anxiety and guilt in the phallic phase and promotes unmanliness. (A. Freud, 1965, p. 210)

Even as these original theories have been tweaked over time, they have continued to hold sway over the psychology of the family: the archetypes of mother, father, and child remain bedrock and are assumed to be the prerequisite of normality. Yet what if there never was a father, just a single mother and a vial of sperm? What if there are no parents of different genders, but two mothers or two fathers? What if the "mother" is a transgender male? What if mother is a virgin, and not one named Mary? What if the mother and father never engaged in sexual intercourse to make their baby? How will the single mother, the virginal mother, the female–female or male–male parent couple, the transgender couple, or the infertile heterosexual couple wrap themselves up in permanent coitus, and why would they when they never had to in the first place for baby to be made? Will babies still hold on to these phantasies when baby is made with the help of some outside party and never as a result of sexual intercourse? Will the parents still unconsciously, or even consciously, position themselves in sexual intercourse even if that is not how their baby came to be?

To make sense of oedipal circles, we need to re-examine our developmental theories built on the assumption of a mother, a father, sexual intercourse, and a child; technology has rendered this assumption anything but universal. If we fail to engage in this re-examination, we will find ourselves jumping to conclusions about the losses to the boy without a father or the confusion for a child with two mothers, before we ever take stock of the data before us. Let us be humbled by the realisation that myth is now reality: there are no storks or cabbage patches, but there are test tubes, Petri dishes, and medical procedures to bring baby to the door; and reality becomes myth if we maintain an obsolete truism that only men and women in sexual union can make a baby.

If we fail to rethink development in the face of assisted reproductive technology, we not only render ourselves out of synch with changing realities; we may create harm by inferring, interpreting, or imposing pathology or loss when there may be none. So, for example, when we insist that all children need a father and will search for one either in reality or fantasy if they are missing one, are we assuming a phylogenetic universality or are we speaking culture-based psycho-social experiences? What is our evidence and what are our data points?

To joggle our thinking, I would like to share a story of two mummies and a baby. Sarah and Mindy were a lesbian couple. They had a baby together, using an anonymous sperm donor and Mindy's egg and womb. Sophia was born, and three years later Mindy was pregnant again with their second child, using the same sperm donor. Sophia was attending a preschool where she was the only child from a two-mother family; every other child had both a mother and a father. At the same time that Mindy became pregnant with their second child, Sarah had come to the realisation that she was transgender and began cross-sex hormone treatment. As she began to get facial hair and her voice deepened, both parents decided it was time to explain to Sophia that Sarah would soon be her daddy rather than her mummy. Cheerfully, they explained that now she would have a daddy like all the other children at school, just like she always said she wanted. In response, Sophia cried out, "But I don't want a daddy, I want my two mummies."

Despite their fantasies, in reality children may very well want what they have, or not want to lose what they have, and not what we or others assume they are missing. When we automatically assume a deficit—as when a child does not have a father, just a sperm donor—we may be projecting our own anxieties about these new-fangled ways of making babies, angst stemming from what I have come to label "reproductive technophobia": our discomfort, prejudices, or un-thought-out aspersions cast on the offspring, parents, and conception participants when a baby is made with the help of a birth other and/or the assistance of medical technology. To staunch the flow of these anxieties, we can turn to the data from Susan Golombok and her colleagues' research on the developmental outcomes for children from birth other families: the children are doing fine, showing healthy development in attachment, relational capacities, social behaviours, identity, and cognitive abilities (Golombok, Murray, Brinsden, & Abdalla, 1999; Golombok, MacCallum, & Goodman, 2001; Golombok & MacCallum, 2003).

Yet aggregate data does not always give us a window into the deeper psyches of the subjects being assessed. Calling on clinical observations in the consultation room, let us now consider the interpersonal and intrapsychic dynamics for both the children and the adults in the new birth oedipal circle. I will be starting from the premise that the concrete conditions of family life deeply alter the developmental trajectories, the internal object relations, and the fantasy lives of children growing up in birth other families. To borrow from Patrick Casement (1992), if there is any time when we need to learn from the patient, rather than from our theories, it is in the stories of the birth other children, in consort with their parents, who are, to quote from Ken Corbett, "looking to us to reach along with them beyond the narrow categories that have shaped our thinking to date" (Corbett, 2009, p. 82).

The birds, the bees, and the birth other story

When Winnicott's model, that there is no baby without a mother (1960, 1971), is extended to accommodate new forms of conception, there is now no baby without all the parties involved in making that baby— genetic parents, social parents, gestational parents, gestational carriers, surrogates, egg donors, sperm donors. As we amend the traditional developmental model based on mother, father, and baby, we also have to discard the traditional birth story for young children: "Mummy and daddy decided we wanted to have a baby. It takes a sperm and an egg to make a baby and then a place for the baby to grow before it is born— that would be inside mummy's womb/uterus. Daddies have sperm. Mummies have eggs. The egg and the sperm have to come together to make a baby. So mummy and daddy put the sperm and egg together to make the baby and then the baby grew inside mummy's womb/uterus. And then out came you."

The expanded story goes something like this: "It takes an egg and a sperm to make a baby and a place for the baby to grow, called a womb or uterus. Men have sperm and women have eggs. Women also have uteruses, and that's why babies grow inside women, and not men, because men don't have uteruses, unless they were once a girl who decided to become a boy later. In some families, the mummy's egg and the daddy's sperm come together to make you. In some families, the mummy doesn't have an egg or the daddy doesn't have sperm, so a woman helps them by giving them an egg or a man helps them by giving them some sperm that mummy and daddy could use to make you. Sometimes, it's both things—the mummy doesn't have an egg and the daddy doesn't have sperm, so another woman and another man help them by giving them both an egg and some sperm so mummy and daddy could have you. In some families, there is only a mummy, she has eggs, but she needs some sperm. So she finds a man who helps by giving some sperm so she could have you. In some families, there is only a mummy and she doesn't have any eggs, and she also needs some sperm, so two different people, a woman and a man, can help her by giving her eggs and sperm so she could have you. In some families, there are two mummies, and they both have eggs, but they need some sperm. So a man helps them by giving them some sperm that come together with one of the mummy's eggs so mummy and mama could have you. The baby also needs a place to grow before she or he comes out. That's called a uterus. In some families, the mummy's uterus can't grow the baby, so another woman helps by letting the baby grow inside her uterus. In some families where there are two mummies, both mummies want to help make the baby, and they can do that, because they can use one mummy's eggs and the other mummy's uterus so you get born, after they get the sperm from the man who is going to help them. In some families, there is only a dad. He needs to find both an egg and a uterus to have a baby. Sometimes that will be the same woman, sometimes it will be two different women—one woman who gives the daddy eggs and another woman who has the baby grow inside her uterus once the egg and sperm come together. Sometimes there will be two dads, and they, too, will need an egg and a uterus for the baby to grow. Like the single dad, sometimes the same woman will give the daddies some eggs for the sperm and also grow the baby in her uterus. Sometimes one woman will give the daddies her eggs and another woman will have the baby grow inside her after they put the egg and sperm together. Sometimes the dads decide that since they both have sperm, they'll mix their sperm together to make their baby, and since it takes only one sperm, they know it won't be both of their sperm but only one of their sperm that made you, but they wanted to do it that way so both daddies got a chance to make you. Sometimes there are daddies who used to be girls and then decided to become a boy, but they kept their uterus and their eggs, but never get to have any sperm, because you have to be born a boy to have sperm. So they are the special daddies who can get pregnant and carry their baby inside them after another man gives them some sperm, maybe the other daddy, if there are two, and that was how you were born."

We have definitely left the land of cabbage patches and storks. If we project into the future, the story will become even more complicated as we develop new technologies, just on the horizon, that allow body cells to be transformed into reproductive material, making it possible for two men or two women to genetically conceive a child together, which may well become reality within the twenty-first century.

I am certainly not advocating telling this whole unwieldy tale to a small child, yet this ever-expanding tale stands as the full and scientifically correct story that informs the new paradigm of the oedipal circle. Psychoanalytic wisdom teaches us that the *fact* of the child's birth other story of origins will not be the deciding factor in developmental outcomes, but rather the metabolism of the fact by the parents, by the culture, and by the child negotiating his or her specific account of conception within the family complex.

Replacing triangles with circles

The psychoanalytic account of oedipal triangles has undergone many renditions. In its original account, the child comes upon the shock that there is not just a mother–child dyad, but a father who has an independent relationship with the mother. Disillusioned, the child discovers the oedipal triangle, in which he or she must negotiate the exclusion from the marital couple's sexual union and the love–hate affair with each of the parents. Developmentally, the discovery of this triangle is crucial for mental development, eventually leading the child to a sexual and gender identity and acceptance of reality.

In contemporary theories, numbers have replaced sex as the crux of oedipal development (Britton, Feldman, & O'Shaugnessy, 1980). The child's discovery of the oedipal triangle is a prototype for *all* human relationships: two can be together; there is a third who looks on. The two are *seen* by the third person. The child is now ready to take the position of the third person. This is crucial for the child's discovery of the world: to be able to observe, to see without panic that things exist outside the child, new things about which the child did not know. So the child learns to look on, to see reality, and not split between objective reality and subjective experience, but rather integrate both domains. As numbers have replaced sex, the very centrality of the oedipal drama as a crux in development has been challenged, yet whether central or not, the child in the birth other family has different challenges in incorporating the additional members in his or her family complex as she or he negotiates the tasks of attachment, individuation, and identity.

With that said, in my clinical work with birth other families, I have found that both numbers and sex go topsy-turvy for the child in the birth other family. The triangle, stretched to a circle, leaves the child in the birth other family with a far more complicated developmental task: negotiating "multiple circulating narratives" (Corbett, 2009, p. 75)—incorporating not just a third, but a fourth, a fifth, and maybe even a sixth, into relational life. When six-year-old Marie is first told, in child-friendly terms, that she was conceived with the help of the nice man who gave mummy and daddy sperm and Marie blurts out, "Oh, Mummy, you did it with someone else!", we are watching in action Marie's creation of a new triangle within the oedipal circle: Marie, Mummy, and the Nice Man. Moving from sharp angles to round circumferences, the oedipal circle becomes an ongoing process over the course of childhood as the son or daughter learns more about the participants in his or her origins and integrates more sophisticated understandings of his or her place in the family complex and the role of each of the players—birth others, parents, and child—in the family drama. Developmental outcomes will be determined not just by the child's feelings about all the players, but also by each of the players' feelings about the child and about each other.

Sex in the circle

By introducing outside thirds (or fourths or fifths) into a most intimate aspect of family life, baby-making, birth other parents are often taken aback by an undercurrent or surge of sexual feelings towards the donor or surrogate—be it sexual desire on the part of the recipient or sexual threat from the recipient's partner (Ehrensaft, 2005). The experience is particularly wrought for parents with a history of infertility—the father who was "shooting blanks" or the mother with broken eggs or a non-working womb can feel particularly threatened about the birth other as the donor or surrogate takes shape in fantasy as both the oedipal victor and sexual predator. The fertile parent, in contrast, as well as the single parent who is missing a partner, may find him- or herself engaging in intense fantasies of running off into the sunset with the donor not as predator, but as idealised sexual object—after all, they did, of sorts, do it together. Enter baby into the midst of these eroticised or tension-filled parental fantasies. Now the child has to deal not just with parents who leave him or her at the bedroom door. He or she has to contend with an adulterous parent who in fantasy did "do it" with someone else, the very someone who helped make baby, and another parent who may be jealous of that nice person who could "do it", usurping the child's position as the excluded third. The child also has to negotiate his or her own feelings about the birth other(s) and each of his or her parents as they show up in embedded triangles, squares, pentagons, even hexagons, within the oedipal circle.

Maureen and Craig had conceived their daughter, Sierra, using a sperm donor from Italy. Seven years after Sierra's birth, Maureen still became dreamy and starry-eyed when she reflected on the donor, whom they would never meet but whom she knew to be a red-haired, blue-eyed attorney from Italy. Craig, a father with insufficient sperm, sat next to her, becoming deflated and morose as he experienced himself the outsider, watching his wife dream about not just any man, but the man who could do what he could not—conceive his child. It was Maureen who was insistent that Sierra not be told the truth about her origins, as she thought the whole process was just "too weird" and worried her daughter would accuse her of adultery. Sierra was finally told the truth about her conception at age fourteen, at the height of her early adolescence, only because Maureen felt pressed into service because she was now worried that Sierra would find out from other adults who already knew and who might unwittingly slip and talk to Sierra about her donor conception. Sierra had myriad reactions, among them some very sensual ones. She found it so romantic that she had a donor from another country, especially Italy, a country populated with gorgeous hunks of men. She spent hours searching on the Internet to learn more about her donor's home city. She wrote a story, "Once there was a man in Arezzo. He grew the garden, and there was this beautiful flower that grew in it. That was Sierra." She read the story aloud, not with the sing-song lilt of a young child, but with a low, sultry voice and the same dreamy look her mother exhibited seven years earlier. Then she grew anxious, worried that her father would feel hurt by the story, maybe even jealous.

At age fourteen, Sierra had to renegotiate her family complex with a fresh series of triangles embedded in a newly discovered circle—herself, mother, and donor; herself, father, and donor; mother, father, and donor; along with a brand-new square: Sierra, mother, father, donor. Because she would never meet her donor, he was ripe to grow even grander as she could shape him into anything she wanted in her erotically tinged fantasies of reproduction, birth, and thirds. So even if no sexual intercourse ever takes place, the dance of the egg and sperm as they create a union and find a womb of their own can create a sexy tale that leaves the child negotiating visions of union, betrayal, and exclusion among multiple partners, a tale co-constructed by the parents' unconscious, or even conscious, transmissions and the child's own internally driven fantasies.

Genetic asymmetry and its toll on the oedipal circle

When one of the intended parents in a two-parent birth other family has a genetic relationship to the child and the other does not, a tug-of-war as to who is a real or legitimate parent can ensue. This is particularly true if the reason for the genetic asymmetry is the medical infertility of one of the two parents (as opposed to social infertility, where neither of the parents' reproductive abilities are compromised, but the two parents are missing one of the gametes to make a baby—the situation in same-sex families). A painful history of infertility can contribute to the non-genetic parent feeling "less than", resulting in either stepping somewhat outside the oedipal circle or being gently shoved off it by the genetic parent, who consciously or unconsciously may indeed perceive him- or herself as the privileged parent.

Yet the socially infertile families are not exempt from this same subtle to overt choreography. Miranda and Rachel sought out therapy for their seven-year-old daughter, Sophie. The therapy was court-mandated, following an arduous custody battle after the two mothers split up. Miranda is Sophie's genetic mother. Sophie was conceived with sperm from a known donor. Rachel, Sophie's non-biological mother, was involved in meeting the donor and was present at the insemination. When Sophie was born, Miranda became a stay-at-home mum and Rachel, a physician, became the full-time breadwinner. Rachel never adopted Sophie. By Rachel's report, she just never got around to it. Miranda, on her part, kept pushing the issue of adoption aside. According to Miranda, Miranda already knew the relationship was doomed to failure by the time Sophie was born and there was no way she was going to let Rachel adopt "her" child. When Sophie was six years old, the two women finally separated, after years of acrimonious tension. Rachel filed for parenting rights. Miranda objected. It went to court soon after the three 2005 California Supreme Court decisions came out that granted parenting rights to lesbian parents who had intended to have a child with their partner and then went on to raise that child, regardless of genetic ties to the child or previous legal standing as a parent. On the basis of that recent legal precedent, Rachel was granted full parentage of Sophie, since she did fit all the stipulated qualifications: as Miranda's long-term partner, she was involved in baby-planning and then participated in the daily care of Sophie within the same household as Miranda for over six years. In face of the court's ruling, Rachel was ecstatic, Miranda apoplectically chagrined.

From Miranda's point of view, Sophie now had no home, had been ripped away from the primary mother she knew and needed, and was exhibiting severe signs of depression and anxiety. As far as Rachel was concerned, Sophie was doing fine, could not be doing better—the only problem was Miranda's overwrought clinginess to Sophie. Even after the court ruling, they carried on with their custody dispute. Rachel wanted more time with Sophie, as much as Miranda had. Miranda felt Rachel already had far more time than was in Sophie's best interests, particularly because Miranda has always been Sophie's primary caretaker and Rachel had functioned more like a traditional father, absorbed in work and around only late evenings and weekends. It is edifying to observe that it is not just the birth other, the outsider, who may be pushed off the oedipal circle by threatened parents; an insider, one of the very parents who intended to have the baby, particularly the one who does not hold genetic credentials, may be at risk for similar exclusion, to the child's detriment.

As for what Sophie wanted for her custody arrangement, "the same, the same with each mum—five days, five days, five days, five days". She made no status differentiation between her genetic and non-genetic mothers—except one lets her have more sweets than the other—and she appeared equally attached to both. Sophie's own placement of her two mothers along the oedipal circle had no bearing on their ongoing tug-of-war with each other. It would be fair to say that Miranda's lack of recognition of the family complex and the inclusive oedipal circle that will be Sophie's to negotiate prevented Miranda from acting in Sophie's best interests.

A specific aspect of two-mother parenting may be at play here. In previous research interviewing men and women in intact families who were committed to sharing the care of their children, I found a trend: based on socially constructed gender socialisation, and perhaps the inevitable divide that women can get pregnant, give birth, and breast-feed, and men cannot, men *do* parenting, while women *are* parents (Ehrensaft, 1987). Using D. W. Winnicott's description of doing versus being (Winnicott, 1971), men more typically experienced parenting as a set of activities and tasks they did among other roles, particularly their work roles. Women, on the other hand, did not experience parenting as a discrete act they could do and then stop doing, but rather a wall-to-wall experience that was at the soul of their being, no matter if they were with their children or apart from them. With that said, if we put two women together and make each of them mothers, the challenges of establishing parity for *both* mothers along the oedipal circle and creating space for both mothers to *be* mothers can be daunting. Genetic asymmetry can only exacerbate this tension.

Yet accounts of attempted bumping off the oedipal circle because of genetic asymmetry are evidenced in heterosexual and two-father families as well. As long as our culture continues to privilege genetic over non-genetic family ties, such genetic asymmetry may be a lethal weapon decimating the intricate weavings of the various geometric shapes that include the intended parents, whether genetically or non-genetically related to the child within the oedipal circle. When any of those inner shapes are destroyed, denied, or compromised, the child is at risk for being left with a void in relatedness or an anxiety about the bonds to one or both intended parents.

Missing pieces and extra pieces

Let us now bring the birth other back into the oedipal circle. For some parents, particularly in two-parent families where one parent has suffered from infertility, genetic asymmetry can be accompanied by a push–pull feeling towards the birth other, that "nice" person who helped baby come to be, as to the birth other's place along the circle.

Amy became a first-time mother at age forty-eight, giving birth to a little girl conceived through in-vitro fertilisation with her husband's sperm and an egg from a known donor and then gestated in Amy's womb. Amy came into therapy when her baby was just under two years old. She explained that she had first tried IVF with her own eggs, and then egg donation, to have her baby.

Amy runs her own small business and is highly successful. Amy had never been anxious to have children, but Benjamin, her husband, some years younger than Amy, was adamant that he wanted children.

Amy's mother, who had been married and divorced several times, delivered an ominous warning: "Don't ruin your life having children." Only at age forty was Amy ready to have a baby. Statistics would say that the odds were against her. But Amy was undaunted: in excellent physical health and looking very young for her years, she was confident that her body would now be as fertile as her mind had always been. But her confidence could not trump her body's failures, so she eventually turned to egg donation.

The search for an egg is a vital part of Amy's entry into mother-hood, leaving a big indentation along the family circle. Amy and Benjamin had an egg donor all picked out. But then, literally at the eleventh hour, Amy found another donor surfing the Internet late at night. Amy "loved" this donor, who fitted all her criteria. She arranged to meet the donor, Judith, and by her own report, they "just hit it off". Soon after, their daughter Maddy was born.

Amy is a take-charge, fast-talking, high-energy, smart, get-to-the-point woman. Yet she lost her verbal footing and broke down in tears in one of her early therapy sessions, blurting out, "I will never lay on Maddy the emotional trips my parents laid on me. How could I ever even think of abandoning her? It's inconceivable."

"Inconceivable" and "abandoning" were key concepts in exploring Amy's feelings of connection to Maddy. Fully acknowledging herself as gestational rather than genetic mother, Amy professed having no strong feelings about her lack of genetic connection to Maddy, and assured me, "I love her to death". Amy echoed the sentiments of many other non-genetic parents, perhaps heartfelt or perhaps a psychological defence to protect from their own sorrow of not having conceived a baby from their own gametes: "Actually, I find it a relief." As Amy saw it, her genetic loadings for psychiatric illness and substance abuse did not look good. With egg donation, she was free of worrying that she would pass those anomalies on to her child. Were these Amy's genuine feelings about her non-genetic relationship with her little girl, or did they function to push away the underlying angst as to whether this baby was really hers or someone else's—Benjamin's, the egg donor's, or Benjamin and the egg donor together as the procreative couple, creating their own family triangle that would leave her in the dust along the circle?

In one session, Amy arrived wincing in pain. She had reinjured the arm that had previously been damaged as a result of giving birth. Amy had arranged a team-building day for her staff, which included bringing in a trapeze artist. As the executive leader far older than any of her staff, Amy pushed herself to do what all the younger women were doing on the trapeze, despite her still-compromised arm mobility. "How could I be so stupid? I just couldn't let all those young little things outdo me." The links to her feelings about the egg donor were inescapable. Amy had just re-enacted, or perhaps was trying to transcend, feelings about her assisted reproductive technology conception: she needed to prove herself to a younger woman with viable eggs that just seem to fly out of her, despite injury to herself from her own swing on the trapeze, that is, her own pregnancy and birth. She also needed to knock that younger woman off the trapeze.

"I just couldn't let all those young little things outdo me" set in motion her rancour and resentment as an older new mother. She railed against people's rude, intrusive comments about her advanced maternal age, particularly when the comments came from younger women, all shadows of the young egg donor with viable eggs to spare. With anger, she spoke of a recent encounter with a young woman at a professional gathering. Amy made mention of her little girl. The young woman replied that her own mother was an older mum, too, and that in middle school she hated it when her mother would pick her up because everyone thought it was her grandmother. Sardonically, Amy asked me, "Now what am I supposed to do with that?" People marvel, they gawk, they think she is a grandmother, they look at her askance for having a baby at forty-eight (in fantasy, she imagines that everyone knows her age). They feel licence to ask if she had trouble getting pregnant, if she used an egg donor. Recently, a stranger asked her, "Were they your eggs?" Simultaneously defiant but yet like a sinner going to confession, Amy admitted that in frustration she did what she promised she would never do—lie. Looking the stranger right in the eye, she responded, "Yes". With some embarrassment, she later told Benjamin what she had done. Completely empathic, he playfully came up with a justification for her response: "Well, the eggs *are* yours. You bought them."

Amy, along with Benjamin, was engaged in a psychological ploy that I have labelled "immaculate deception", conception and birth narratives that either stretch the truth or blatantly distort reality to assuage parents' anxieties in the face of their own internal misgivings and external disapprobation for transcending nature and calling on scientific methods and outside parties to make a baby. Amy was not fabricating the curious or spurious questioning that has come her way upon being perceived as a "too old" woman carrying a baby, either in her womb or in her arms—it is a social reality reported by many older mothers. At the same time, Amy admitted to her own vulnerability, having a very thin skin regarding people's comments about her older and egg donor motherhood that she feels was none of their business and for which she had no appropriate language to reply. She was also terrified that she would transfer her discomfort to Maddy, not just her own reactivity to people's responses but her own internalised angst about being a "too old" egg donor mother.

Enter the egg donor. Amy's conflict about her advanced maternal age gets knotted up with her resentments towards the egg donor, feelings she believed she was not entitled to. Amy expressed feeling grateful towards Judith, the young woman with whom she immediately bonded and who made it possible for her to bear and rear Maddy. She even had taken to going on Facebook to see photographs and find out more about Judith. Recall that the Internet is the very place Amy first found Judith in the eleventh hour. Yes, Amy would never "friend" Judith on Facebook—that would be too intrusive. Amy expressed discomfort with her own entangled emotions directed at Judith: "I just feel so guilty about being mad at this person I just love and who I couldn't have had Maddy without. I should feel thankful to this twenty-seven-year-old woman who was able to produce *nineteen* good eggs, all nineteen fertilised by Benjamin's sperm." Then, like a child when the teacher leaves the room, Amy became raucous, laughing, "Yeah, that little twenty-seven-year-old bitch." She could no longer contain the rage and sexual jealousy towards this younger woman who produced eggs like they were water flowing from a fountain and who joined in a union with her younger husband and *his* fertile gametes that created not just one but several viable embryos from those nineteen golden eggs. In her frenzied fantasies, as far as she was concerned regarding the egg donor's fate: "Off with her head" and "Kick her out of the circle".

Hard as Amy tried to reduce the egg donor to an object rather than a member of the oedipal circle, to the eggs that are hers because she bought them, the defence did not work. In Amy's inner life, the donor with the nineteen golden eggs, with whom she has no ongoing contact, had her angel wings ripped off, got knocked off the circle, and reared her ugly head as she reminds Amy of her own eggs' failure and her medically engineered motherhood that kept getting exposed every time her advanced age led someone to probe, "Your eggs?"

That was the push part, and now the pull. Watching her cousin, Sandy, and her female partner give birth to a baby with the help of a friend's sperm, a friend who became an intimate part of the family, Amy now had longings for Judith to become a part of her family just like Sandy's donor did for Sandy's family. She envied her cousin and partner—they had a donor who would actually be a real person in their child's life. Now she fantasised Judith taking interest in Maddy. She went to Facebook in search of more information about the egg donor, not just to find reflections of her little girl's genetic self but in search of someone who could become an active member of the oedipal circle, even taking the place of a grandmother who showed no interest in Amy's baby. So now the egg donor now resides in Amy's mind as both an idealised fairy godmother and an envied goose with endless golden eggs, neither one of which is a good fit as a real participant along the oedipal circle.

For other families, there is a missing piece—either a second parenting partner or a parent of a particular gender. In these families, we can witness more of the pull without the push—seeking, sometimes delusionally, sometime desperately, to activate the birth other as an oedipal circle participant. For example, Jason and Ken had two daughters, Felicia, age four and a half, and Grace, age four months. Unlike Amy, who experienced medical infertility, these two fathers confronted the other kind of infertility, social—they were missing a body with the necessary other gametes to make a baby. The two girls were conceived with Jason's sperm and eggs from a donor known to the fathers, after finding her through an agency and subsequently identifying her through a Facebook page. Each girl was carried by a different surrogate. When Felicia was born, Sarah, the donor, took an active interest in the baby, wanting to see pictures and get updates about how Felicia was doing. Both fathers were more than happy to accommodate her, although Ken, the non-genetic parent, was more hesitant and had some questions about Jason's investment in keeping Sarah so actively in the picture. Didn't Felicia already have all the parents she needed?

When Jason and Ken decided to have a second child, they turned to Sarah again, wanting both their children to be fully genetically related (Jason was to be the genetic father again). By this time, Sarah was now engaged to be married and her interest in hearing news about Felicia had notably dwindled. Her fiancé was not thrilled about Sarah being an egg donor again, but Sarah went forward anyway, as she needed the money, and the fathers were only too happy to go forward so they could assure a full genetic connection between their daughters and because they felt confident in Sarah as a donor. Both fathers were very firm in their desire to allow the girls access to Sarah over the course of their lives. But when Grace was born, there was not a word from Sarah. Soon after, however, they received a letter from Sarah's fiancé. He was demanding that Ken and Jason's daughters make no contact with Sarah and that the fathers stay out of his and Sarah's family life. By his report, he and Sarah wanted no connection between the children they hoped to have and the two girls conceived with Sarah's eggs and Jason's sperm.

Jason and Ken were devastated, not for themselves, but for their daughters. They struggled to sort out how they could either pull Sarah back in to the circle or begin explaining to Felicia and later to Grace their complicated family complex with a donor who shunned interest and, additionally, two surrogates who, according to the fathers, did it only for the money and then absented themselves. They felt a particular urgency because Felicia, right on the mark developmentally, had just come to them and asked, "Daddy, Papa, whose tummy did I come from?"

Jason and Ken desperately wanted a birth other in their family circle—the egg donor. But her life circumstances had changed, and there was now a tangential line running out from the circle—another man claiming the egg donor as his own and not wanting intruders in his own family matrix that he planned to build with Sarah. Perhaps these visions of circle inclusion had not been mapped out sufficiently among all the adults before Grace and Felicia were born. There is also a glaring exclusion of two other members of the oedipal circle—the surrogates, who were being pushed off the circle just as Sarah was being pulled in. All of these oedipal circle conundrums were brought by the innocent question of an inquisitive little girl: "Daddy and Papa, whose tummy did I come from?", which brings us to the last consideration: the activity of the children along the family circle.

Kidnappers and kings and queens

What about the special role of the birth other in relation to the parents in the child's fantasy life? With the goal of solidifying parent–child ties, I hold the position that the birth other should not be referred to as a mother or father. Those terms should be reserved for the individuals who intended to have a baby with the help of an outside party or those individuals who end up raising that baby. Yet that, of course, is not how the children may see it as they do their own internal work to find a place for the donor or surrogate in the oedipal circle.

Birth other parents are often taken aback to discover that once their baby arrives, the nice man or woman who helped them conceive or gestate their baby is suddenly transformed in fantasy into a conniving kidnapper who will scheme to take their baby away and claim it as their own. Such occurrences, although rare, have actually occurred, and when they do, they typically make national and international headlines, and certainly do not go unnoticed by birth other mothers and fathers who follow the news. But even with no such media intrusion, the fact of including an outsider into the intimacy of baby-making and the fact that this outsider might leave a permanent genetic stamp on their child can compromise a parent's secure feeling of bonding and attachment to the child, particularly for the non-genetic parent. If not actually laying claim to the baby, the birth other may nonetheless steal the child's affections, creating a new oedipal square of parents, child, and birth other as evil other. This fear of birth other as kidnapper or interloper can occur regardless of whether the birth other is anonymous or a close family member. Out of fear, the parents' remedy may be to ban the birth other from thought, discourse, or presence in the family. Another psychological defence is to do a sleight of mind and reduce the donor or surrogate to a vial of sperm, eggs in a dish, or a disembodied womb, depersonalising the birth other, turning him or her into a part-object, and thus eradicating the feared interloper from the oedipal circle.

Whatever the defensive manoeuvres, parents' anxious fantasies about the birth other as kidnapper or interloper, if left unmetabolised, may then be transmitted to the child, challenging the child's own sense of belonging and permanence. Corbett (2009) reported on a two-mother family in which the mothers attempted to place the anonymous sperm donor out of consciousness as soon as their child was born. In turn, their seven-year-old son Andy "had it in mind that he could not meet this man until he was eighteen; otherwise, this man might want to keep him" (Corbett, 2009, p. 62). A patient of mine, Caroline, was not told the truth of her anonymous sperm donor origins until age eight. Before that, her father was too frightened that he would lose his daughter's affections to this man whose identity could easily be found out as he was secured through mutual friends. Only when he felt his bonds with his daughter were secure enough was he able to agree to reveal to his daughter the truth that he was not her genetic father. Soon after being told, Caroline created a dark, dismal fantasy in which a strange man came and spirited her away from her mother and father, leaving her to live a cold, lonely life on the top of a mountain.

Within the oedipal circle, the child, making sense of his or her genetic and gestational roots, may need to create in fantasy a birth other who truly wants him or her, rather than one who callously gives gametes away or loans out a womb and then walks away. Simultaneously, reaching to find his or her place in the family and challenged by too many players, the child may, like the parents, feel a need to expel the birth other from the family circle and transform him or her into an evil other in order to maintain the traditional triangle—only intentional parents need apply.

In the traditional oedipal triangle, the child grows anxious about his or her fantasies of stealing one of the parents from the other parent, fearing retribution, punishment, even genital mutilation, if he or she should steal either mummy or daddy from the other parent. Yet in the birth other oedipal square, or pentagon or hexagon, if there are two or three birth others involved, it is the child, not the parent, who may be stolen away, either in body or in love, a fantasy that may be mutually held by both parent and child. For the birth other child, the fear may be not so much one of fantasised annihilation, but one of being spirited away, leaving no parents to either fall in love with or learn to be a third with. In that case, it may very well serve the child well to dispense with the conniving kidnapper so as to get on with the tasks of individuation, identity, and belonging with their primary attachment figures—their parents.

Alternatively, the child, in fantasy, may bring the birth other in within a whole other geometric configuration. Particularly as the child grows older, the birth other can be transformed once again—from the nice man or woman of the earliest stories to the conniving kidnapper to the wonderful king or queen who will bring the child fame and fortune. The child traverses around the oedipal circle and lands on the birth other as the key player in what we know as the latency-age family romance, when the child dreams of an idealised family in which now her own parents need not apply.

Deanna, age ten, had been told early on by her parents that she was conceived with the help of an anonymous egg donor. She began to wonder about her donor. Deanna was an excellent basketball player. She imagined her egg donor was as well. Certainly, her parents could neither dribble nor shoot a basket. Deanna was pleased with her long, swan-like neck. Both her parents had short, squat necks, so she must have inherited her lovely neck from her donor. She fantasised about her future: she and her donor would meet in a café. They would fall into each other's arms, overwhelmed with emotion. They would be awed by their strong physical resemblance. Deanna would be at Harvard then, studying biology. Her egg donor would already be a well-known scientist. They'd move in together and become a rich and famous duo. All her classmates who ignored Deanna at school would suddenly be clamouring for her affection and attention. They would be begging to meet her famous egg donor. Deanna's fantasy is emblematic of yet another square within the circle: a move towards independence from her parents and an identification and longing for the donor who is responsible for half the child's genetic make-up, as the child leaves her gestational mother and genetic father to their more mundane, boring existence.

By introducing the birth other into the oedipal circle, children are caught on the horns of a dilemma. If told the truth about their origins, there will be times in their lives when they will want to know who the birth other is and feel free to fantasise about the person or people who were so instrumental in bringing them into being; yet they may feel constricted in pursuing those desires for fear of fraying the bonds of love with their parents. There may be still another force pulling on the children—the conscious or unconscious psychodynamics of the birth others, as they may also be engaging in their own reveries or desires regarding the offspring conceived with the aid of their gametes or wombs.

Clinical observations and research data all indicate that children's primary attachments and identifications are with their parents, the people who nurture them, whether genetically connected or not. These very attachments and identifications are the source of the children's fears of hurting their parents or even losing them if they think about, fantasise, or wish to search out their birth other(s). These fears do not develop from thin air. Parents can indeed respond to their children's curiosity about or involvement with the birth other with subtle to overt discomfort or dread, reverting back to their early fears of the birth other as conniving kidnapper, as they observe their children grow and develop more sophisticated understandings of their birth other origins or more elaborated mental connections to the birth other and to the birth other's placement along the oedipal circle.

Parents play a critical role in facilitating a solution to the child's dilemma. By opening up a space for a family reverie, in which parents and children together share their thoughts and fantasies about the birth other, and by allowing the children private space to engage in their independent family romances that might include the birth other, the children will feel their parents' support and have the freedom to weave together a tapestry that includes all the members of the oedipal circle (Ehrensaft, 2007). In round-robin fashion, the parents will in turn discover the permanence of their children's bonds to them and the resilience of the family they have built with the aid of assisted reproductive technology.

The whole, part, and two-headed birth other

Although each family will need to make its own decisions as to if and when to tell their child about their birth other origins, it is my recommendation, gleaned from the wisdom of the adoption field, that children be told the truth about their birth other origins, preferably early in life before they shape erroneous notions of their genetic or gestational connections. The children will benefit from this information as it provides them with both an accurate medical history, increasingly advantageous in an era of discoveries of genetic contributions to health and disease, and a psychologically authentic narrative of their personal and family life.

For those children who are not told, the birth other still remains in the minds of the parents, sometimes leaking out, as when a non-genetic parent looks away with discomfort when a passing stranger asks, "So who does your baby look like, anyway?" In the situations of nondisclosure, the children may still be metabolising their birth other origins in the form of the "unthought blown", a feeling or intuition about their assisted reproductive technology conception emanating from their parents' subconscious or unconscious transmission of information (Ehrensaft, 2007). Lastly, for those children who are told only later about the participation of egg donors, sperm donors, surrogates, or gestational carriers in their procreation, a renegotiation of critical developmental tasks concerning belonging, attachment, and identity will be in order as their oedipal triangle is newly discovered to be a circle with all its embedded configurations.

If birth others are not parents, who are they to a child? We are a culture that privileges genetic roots, and in that context, birth other children, in contemplating their donor or surrogate, are in search not of a parent but a reflection of self. They not only have to find a place for the donor, surrogate, or gestational carrier along the oedipal circle; they also have to construe a whole image and definition of that person and a concept of themselves that includes the participation of that outside person in their very being.

The impulses of parents or the culture at large to reduce the birth other to a vial of sperm, eggs in a dish, or a disembodied womb rarely work, and if they do, transforming the donor or surrogate into a part-object is typically at the expense of the children's opportunities to explore the full terrain of the people who made them and the people who raise them. At the same time, the desire to create a whole parent when there is none, more typically evident in single-parent or same-sex birth other families missing a second parent or a parent of the opposite gender respectively, is also an artifice. If we watch the children do their own work, what we observe is that they are not content to leave the birth other as a part-object presence, nor do they want to artificially transform the donor into a fully fledged parent, but instead they do their own creative work to establish hybrid birth others and hybrid selves in the context of their own birth stories.

Caroline, the girl left on the cold, lonely mountain by the conniving kidnapper, later in adolescence learned the identity of her sperm donor and began baby-sitting for his children, her genetic half-siblings. She began referring to this man as her "bio". Colin and Aja were twins born to Cathey, a single mother, with aid of both a sperm donor and an egg donor. The twins were told of their sperm donor origins early in life, but only later of their egg donor conception, a phenomenon not uncommon as mothers struggle more with their angst about a competing egg than about the missing sperm. Despite her careful language about Julie, the nice lady who helped by giving her eggs, Aja began announcing to others that she had another mother, and wondered, on Mother's Day: "Should I make a card for Julie, too? It's kind of like I have two mums." Colin approached Cathey and asked about himself and his twin sister, "So, do we have three genes—yours, Mark's, and Julie's?" Madeline was another single mother in the same position as Cathey—an older single mother using both a sperm donor and an egg donor to conceive her son, Matthew. She, too, was hesitant to tell Matthew that he was not conceived with her egg, but finally decided to do so when he was five. Curiously, he looked at Madeline and asked, "So who do I look like?" Madeline found herself engaging in the same three-pronged creation reverie as little Colin's as she responded: "Well, all three of us." She sheepishly explained: "I didn't think that was stretching the truth. There's phenotype and everything."

It is the "everything" that is of interest here—drawing the oedipal circle in such a way that despite scientific evidence or reality-based family narratives, donors are assigned parent status, non-genetic parents are given genotype privilege, and baby in fantasy holds the genes of not two but three or more people. In negotiating the triangles, squares, and more complicated geometric shapes within the oedipal circle, we watch the children take the concrete reality of their conception and integrate it with the emotional realities of their own family life and their unique internal psychological constructions to create a self who feels whole and complete and a relational matrix that includes all the people who made them and all the people who raise them. So now, when Matthew says goodnight to Madeline, he sings out, "Goodnight, Mummy/ Daddy".

Will the circle be unbroken?

The child will do as well as all the family members together in being able to contemplate, metabolise, and think through the shared reality of their constructed birth other family and deal with the complicated matrices within their oedipal circle. Over time, the birth other child will continually reprocess the information with each leap in cognitive or emotional development. Sasha was told at an early age that her mummy and daddy made her with the help of an egg donor, who also happened to be her mother's niece, Jessica. When Sasha was five years old, Jessica, now married, was pregnant with her own child, Fiona. Sasha, when told about Fiona, was confused: "You mean Jessica has more than one egg?" At age six, Sasha asked, "So, Mum, am I adopted?" A year later, Sasha asked her mother, "So, is Jessica my mum?" Then two years later, as if a light bulb went off, Sasha turned to her mother and exclaimed, "So wait a minute. Isn't Fiona my sister?" Mummies, daddies, donor, donor's eggs, donor's sibling all reverberate within Sasha's evolving oedipal circle, a twenty-first-century phenomenon that could never be foreseen in an early twentieth-century ditty, "Just Molly and Me and Baby makes three".

Note

1. The first known sperm donor baby was reported in 1884, performed by Dr William Pancoast of Jefferson Medical College. He impregnated the wife of an infertile man with sperm from a medical student. The wife remained unaware of the procedure, being told that the doctor was performing a simple gynaecological surgery. The sperm was acquired through a contest among Dr Pancoast's medical students, perhaps we could say for the most studly sperm.

References

Britton, R., Feldman, M., & O'Shaughnessy, E. (1980). *The Oedipus Complex Today: Clinical Implications*. London: Karnac.

Casement, P. J. (1992). *Learning from the Patient*. New York: Guilford.

Corbett, K. (2009). *Boyhoods: Rethinking Masculinities*. New Haven: Yale University Press.

Ehrensaft, D. (1987). *Parenting Together: Men and Women Sharing the Care of Their Children*. New York: The Free Press.

Ehrensaft, D. (2005). *Mommies, Daddies, Donors, Surrogates*. New York: Guilford.

Ehrensaft, D. (2007). The stork didn't bring me, I came from a dish: psychological experiences of children conceived through assisted reproductive technology. *Journal of Infant, Child, and Adolescent Psychotherapy, 6(2)*: 124–140.

Ehrensaft, D. (2008a). It ain't over until the fat lady sings: commentary on *Wherefore the Oedipus Complex in Adolescence*, by Marsha H. Levy-Warren. *Studies in Gender and Sexuality, 9(4)*: 349–364.

Ehrensaft, D. (2008b). When baby makes three or four or more: attachment, individuation, and identity in assisted-conception families. In: R. A. King, S. Abrams, A. S. Dowling, & P. M. Brinich (Eds.), *The Psychoanalytic Study of the Child, Volume 63* (pp. 3–23). New Haven: Yale University Press.

Freud, A. (1965). *Normality and Pathology in Childhood*. New York: International Universities Press.

Glass, J. (2003). *Three Junes*. New York: Anchor Books.

Golombok, S., & MacCallum, F. (2003). Practitioner review: outcomes for parents and children following non-traditional conception: what do clinicians need to know? *Journal of Child Psychology and Psychology, 44*: 303–315.

Golombok, S., MacCallum, F., & Goodman, E. (2001). The "test-tube" generation: parent–child relationships and the psychological well-being of in-vitro fertilization children at adolescence. *Child Development, 72*: 599–608.

Golombok, S., Murray, C., Brinsden, P., & Abdalla, H. (1999). Social vs. biological parenting: family functioning and the social-emotional development of children conceived by egg or sperm donation. *Journal of Child Psychology and Psychiatry, 40*: 519–527.

Hinshelwood, R. D. (1989). *A Dictionary of Kleinian Thought*. Northvale, New Jersey: Jason Aronson.

Winnicott, D. W. (1960). The theory of the parent–infant relationship. In: *The Maturational Processes and the Facilitating Environment* (pp. 37–55). Madison, CO: International Universities Press, 1965.

Winnicott, D. W. (1971). *Playing and Reality*. London: Tavistock.

CHAPTER THREE

Psychoanalytic treatment of anxiety related to motherhood and the use of assisted reproductive technology

Terese Schulman

Introduction

For several decades, a striking worldwide demographic shift has occurred in the United States and all developed countries. Women are waiting longer to have children. The average maternal age of one-third of women giving birth to a first child in the United States is thirty. The proportion of first live births to women over thirty-five has increased nearly eight times since 1970. Those using assisted reproductive technology (ART) in 1970 accounted for one in one thousand births; presently, its use has increased to one in twelve births (Covington & Burns, 2006).

The women's movement of the 1960s and 1970s highlighted women's inequality to men in the workplace and the inequality of expectations in the home. Important changes were promoted, such as equal pay, equality in promotion, and increased participation by men in the home and in parenting. The economic independence of women, increased longevity, as well as the promise of high-tech assisted reproductive techniques if problems with conception arose, has influenced more women to delay marriage and motherhood.

I have noticed a phenomenon in my practice over the years involving women who originally enter treatment because of their difficulty finding a meaningful and lasting love relationship. A good number of these women have gone on to reveal a lack of sexual satisfaction and a hesitation to consider motherhood. Many of them come in at an age when the limits of fertility are approaching.

I will begin by discussing this constellation of complaints and the common features shared by this group of women in relation to their mothers. I will then illustrate the way some of these conflicts appeared clinically through material from the psychoanalytic treatment of two patients and will show that the issues that had caused them to delay pregnancy re-emerged as they decided to use in-vitro fertilisation.

Conflicts and anxieties about motherhood

When the decision to be a mother is conflicted, there are innumerable ways to avoid conscious knowledge about the anxiety that surrounds the decision. Some of the women who delay speak about their wish for a child in the future, while imagining that a few more years of work to secure the down-payment on a house will be all they need before trying to become pregnant. A woman may take up a demanding professional course of study that will result in an additional degree or qualification to ensure future success when she has her child. If having a child with a partner is important, the search for a partner can become the focus in a way that obviates thinking beyond that to parenthood. While these women may declare an unambivalent intention to have a child, their method stalls any movement in that direction.

Other women unconsciously use the societal trend of delaying childbirth to deepen the cover under which their unconscious fears about having a child reside. Denying the window of time in which they are fertile, they may never really declare their wish for a child, but contend that they need to continue working to avoid having their career suffer, a statement that does unfortunately frame a real dilemma faced by many women today. However, the women in this group don't ever face their ambivalence about motherhood; instead, they use the permission to delay found in the message about women's need for equality of opportunity.

The result for these women is that by the time they try to conceive, their fertility may be reduced because of age or, regardless of age, because of unexpected physical complications that further delay conception. Some give up on motherhood altogether, while others turn to adoption or assisted reproductive technologies, both of which can be emotionally and financially expensive.

Identification and internalisation

There were noticeable similarities in the way the group of women whom I previously described as coming for help because of their difficulty finding a love relationship describe their mothers. They described the disjunction between the love their mothers expressed for them and what they felt to be their lack of emotional availability. Common descriptors of their mothers included "critical", "depressed", "frustrated", and "felt under-appreciated". Because of the mothers' perceived unavailability, the women felt they weren't worthy of notice and concluded that their own wishes were too much for anyone. They denied or trivialised what they needed in order to conform to how little effort their mother seemed to want to expend on them.

When they did feel angry, demanding, or resentful towards their mothers, this group of women experienced tremendous turmoil over whether their anger was reasonable. They then used these very strong feelings as evidence that they were overly sensitive or "troubled". They were frightened of any impatience or anger they felt, fearful of hurting their mother, whom they not only perceived as unavailable but as damaged because of the very features that interfered with the mother–daughter relationship.

As treatment proceeded, this group of women often came to recognise their mothers were jealous of their other relationships or envious of their accomplishments. Recognition of these reactions both shook their faith in themselves and their mothers, while simultaneously validating an element of the dissatisfaction they experienced in relationship to their mothers.

It is important to remember that the mothers described by the women in my sample represent internal objects, rather than objective pictures of their mothers. Internal objects are made up of both subjective perceptual experiences as well as fantasies about oneself and others, mediated by one's habitually preferred mechanisms of defence. Internal objects form the basis of the unconsciously experienced feelings we all have of the "presence of the object" (Sandler,

1990, pp. 871–873). Central to my understanding of the trouble that many of the women in my practice had in achieving marriage, sexual satisfaction, and a baby, was the problematic nature of their internalised maternal object.

Developmental context

Developmentally, the experience of pregnancy and childbirth is a continuation of the ongoing psychological task of separating from one's mother. The goal is to become an adult, able to conduct and responsible for her own life. Early in a girl's normal development, the mother is experienced as a powerful, life-giving figure who is well-enough attuned to her baby and with whom the girl gets pleasure through feelings of merger. As development continues, a complex identification along with patterns of defence are laid down. Sexual intercourse is one way that a girl establishes that her body is her own, not her mother's (Pines, 2012). During pregnancy, a woman re-experiences identifying with her pre-oedipal mother. A pleasurable feeling of unity with her mother is felt because she now carries a developing baby in her, as her own mother carried her years ago. She may also experience identifying with the baby and imagine what it had been like to be carried in her mother's body. For women who have had a good experience with their mothers, this kind of regression can feel pleasurable because the identification is with a mother who was generous and attuned (Pines, 2012).

Women who are not pregnant also fantasise about what a future pregnancy would be like for them, informed by unconscious memories of their experience with their mothers in infancy. For women whose experience with their mothers has not been "good enough"—that is, their relationship was one in which there was too much frustration, rage, or neglect, and subsequent guilt—the threat of experiencing a regression to identifying with their internal mother in pregnancy can be frightening and unwanted (Pines, 2012).

Although the presence of ambivalent feelings is the norm for any mother, these women fear the ambivalence that accompanies their fantasies. There are numerous possibilities that make a woman with this background hesitate to carry a pregnancy, some of which I'll enumerate in order to show the breadth and seriousness of the threat these women can feel.

1. Rejected by her mother, a woman may imagine a developing baby in her as an unwanted part of herself and feel quite rejecting of her developing foetus.
2. For some women, an unconscious fear of being their mother's rival moves them to avoid pregnancy altogether, and even abort a pregnancy (Pines, 2012). They do so because they fear that their baby will be seen as *their* achievement, with damaging consequences to their mother.
3. The baby can be pictured as a demanding, needy person that can never be satisfied, mirroring the relationship that the woman had with her mother.
4. Finally, a woman can fear that she is or will become like her mother and make her baby suffer in the way she suffered.

The negative feelings the women in my sample experienced when thinking of having their own baby aroused a fear of loss because they imagined their attitude would result in their being an inadequate mother and hurting their child. The severe guilt felt due to this worry can diminish the protective quality of one's good object (Parker, 1997). The function of a good object is to:

> … produce a sense of there being a good, helpful figure inside …
> The good internal object provides the continual internal dialogue of
> encouragement and self-esteem on which confidence and psycho-
> logical security is based. (Hinshelwood, 1989, p. 142)

Feelings of inadequacy can be a breeding ground for hatred towards a baby, which heightens the anxiety about one's mothering and then decreases enjoyment of the baby. Women who have had more depriving experiences with their mothers can lack the confidence to feel that as a mother they will experience themselves as a good and loving person who can nurture their baby. Motherhood can look like too big a risk. It should be said that for some women, given their traumatic pasts, this judgement is probably the correct one.

Shared by the group of women I'm discussing was their concern about their unsatisfying sexual lives, a concern that they all eventually raised. Here again, the nature of the internalised mother, along with other major caretakers, plays a role in a child's sexual development, because the attitude an adult has about sex and the ease with which one can freely participate in sexual activity with an appropriate partner are linked to her perception of the availability of her parents and major caretakers. Mitchell states that in normal adult sex, "… the mutual exchange of intense pleasure and emotional responsiveness is perhaps the most powerful medium in which emotional connection and intimacy is sought, established, lost and regained" (Mitchell, 1988, p. 107). For the women I focus on in this chapter, anxiety about their partners' emotional unavailability made each sexual contact and the prospect of intimacy and dependence very risky. Various attempts to diminish this risk were developed. Some women tended to attach themselves to unavailable men, while others avoided sexual relationships altogether. Still others engaged in intercourse and only simulated enjoyment.

As the issues I've outlined are worked through, some women then decide they want to have children. They may be unable to use their own eggs to achieve a pregnancy, or a different fertility problem is found, and this is where discussion about ART enters the picture.

The clinical examples that follow show the process that can unfold in therapy to help work through the conflicts and then some of the difficulties that accompany the use of ART.

Case of Clare

Clare was forty years old when she came to treatment. Trained as a professional in a male-dominated field, she had recently been hired to take a demanding position that required using slightly different skills than she knew to be her strong suit. She hoped that her boss would help her. Their relationship was highly flirtatious which, I was to hear, continued a long-standing pattern with male employers.

As we worked, she realised that she was constantly undermining herself by flirting with her boss, and at the same time, was not working to get her own clients because she was afraid he might see her as a rival. This fear of being seen as a rival extended to her male co-workers as well, although she also feared that they underestimated her because she was a woman.

This led her to talk about her concern that she was never with men whom she wanted to marry or with whom she wanted to have children. Instead, she often dated "nice" men for a few years who weren't ambitious enough for her; they were not men she wanted to marry.

Clare was the youngest child. Clare described her mother as being beautiful, with a good social life and varied interests, but whom she also characterised as depressed, unappreciated, and unfulfilled by her role as mother and homemaker; as we spoke more about her childhood, Clare began to appreciate how much more attention she had wanted from her mother.

Her mother could be quite nasty and critical when things weren't done her way. She described family life as rough and combative, mainly because of her brothers' competition with each other. She felt that her mother did not impose enough limits on their rough play; in an early vignette, she described how one of her brothers purposely tripped her as she raced to catch a ball.

Clare's response to that competitiveness was by trying to keep up with them; having to prove herself equal to men was a theme that continued to plague her. She didn't want to be like her mother, whom she saw as denigrated by her brothers and sister; her attempts to be as good as her brothers also contained a wish to rescue her mother and be her champion.

Clare portrayed her father, a professional in the same field as she, as a gentle, soft-spoken man who, at times, had a playful sparkle in his eye, and who seemed bewildered by his wife's complaints about his unavailability. Clare was the favourite of both of her parents, garnering resentment from her siblings and making her feel fearful and guilty. In order to stave off her anxiety and "deserve" the favoured status, she tried to do everything perfectly and worked incessantly.

Sex was difficult for Clare because she was so tense. Some foreplay could be pleasurable but then she would "freeze up" and her excitement would disappear.

As we worked, Clare became more aware that her relationships were only with men whom she couldn't marry. Once she had this realisation, she stopped engaging in those relationships. Subsequently, she realised she was lonely. She began dating men who were more suitable for marriage and fatherhood, and did become involved with the man whom she eventually married. However, fears that she would be trapped into a degrading second-best position if she continued her involvement with him were prevalent. She remained competitive with him and vigilant about whether or not he loved her.

The elements of Clare's oedipal conflict ran throughout her treatment. Rivalry and competition, winning and being beaten, were struggles that interfered with her most important relationships. When I first met her, she was competing with her boss and co-workers; in the background was the wife of her boss. Her parents, who called her their "white light", favoured her, and she thought her father favoured her over her mother. These "victories", while somewhat gratifying, left her feeling uneasy, a feeling that ran through all of her relationships. She examined others' behaviours for evidence of envy or revenge. This, we discovered, was an expression of guilt about her own rivalrous feelings and actions of her own that she could see were hurtful towards others. Her guilt about being favoured had caused her to feel uncertain about what she could legitimately have, which included marriage, sex, children of her own, and satisfaction with her life. She worked hard, with little enjoyment or relaxation, in order to justify her favoured status.

The theme of competition and rivalry was prevalent in the transference–countertransference. Clare accused me at times of having critical thoughts about her, and would parse my tone of voice for any impatience she was sure I was having about her "slow" progress. She also found me helpful, which endeared me to her, but then made her afraid of being my "puppet". Feeling vulnerable, she would suddenly become angry and be critical of me. These moments would come on very suddenly and forcefully, sometimes leaving me unable to think momentarily, not unlike what I'd imagined Clare felt when her mother got angry.

Through examining these moments with me, as well as her interactions with the man she eventually married, Clare began to understand how she protected herself against fear of the devastation she would feel if she lost either of us. Her fear seemed to be triggered by a belief that enjoying someone deserved punishment, as if her love was shutting rivals out. Her affection for me was tainted by the fear that she couldn't also love the man with whom she was involved and put him first. It was as if she could only love one person at a time. After a long time in which she vacillated between loving him and backing away from him by wondering if he was the best she could do, she began to feel more confident about her desire to be with him and they decided to marry.

Clare felt that she wanted to be a mother, but only inside a marriage. Once she was engaged, she often talked about looking into adoption or using a surrogate, knowing she was no longer fertile. However, she continued to delay investigating either option. Some of our work on her hesitation had to do with her concern, expressed in the transference, about what she could legitimately have, in comparison to what I had or did not have. If I wasn't a mother, she reasoned, she would be surpassing me and that might make me envious, making me an unreliable source of help. If I did have a child, she imagined me adopting a condescending attitude that would convey disdain about all of her excitement. The issue of rivalry and envy again frightened her into delay.

Clare finally took the lead and actively moved forward on her wish to have a child. Throughout most of her analysis, Clare had only considered using adoption. Using a surrogate had been judged as too expensive. Quite suddenly, Clare began to talk about using a donor ovum and carrying the pregnancy. The manner in which she spoke about this alternative made it sound as if she were considering it because it was the best cost-saving measure available. She had to "sneak" what she wanted into plain sight, hoping to hide her excitement from me and the other fantasied disapproving and envious figures in her mind.

Once she felt that she was entitled to her wish to be pregnant, she delayed the process again for several months while she embarked on a search for reassurance that the use of ART wasn't against the teachings of her religion. Next, she wondered whether or not to ask a younger family member to be the ovum donor, giving her child some genetic connection to her and her family. However, Clare finally realised, amid the turmoil about whom to pick or leave out, that she wanted *no one* from her family to serve as donor, and by carrying the pregnancy, she wanted to make the baby as close as was possible, a creation of just her and her husband. Consideration of family members had been out of guilt about leaving them out, which she feared would earn their disapproval about making a move to rival them, by forming her own family.

She and her fiancé chose a donor and a pregnancy followed. They married. A healthy child arrived soon after.

Case of Paula

Paula came to treatment because she was unable to recover from the upset she felt after being jilted by a man with whom she had been having an affair. The abrupt way he ended the affair was especially troubling to her because she had believed he felt a lot for her. His sudden withdrawal made her wonder whether she had just imagined his caring for her at all. Had she misunderstood from the beginning?

The other issue that plagued her was fear that this man broke the relationship off because he sensed that something was wrong with her. She characterised herself as having little sexual interest in most men. When she did feel attracted to a man, she experienced an intense sexual craving that she often gave into. The men were more likely to initiate the break-up. This she understood to be a result of her lack of something other women had which both attracted men and made them stay attached. Paula stated that she wanted to marry and have children; her inability to attract and to keep men interested in her was very painful.

Paula was the eldest of four children; she was four years older than her twin brothers and six years older than her youngest brother. She described feeling close to her father before the birth of her twin brothers, but afterwards she felt he stopped paying attention to her. It was clear to me that she felt he deserted her. Subsequent to this one-time recitation to me about her close relationship with her dad, she always described her father as having been boring, grumpy, or just generally disconnected.

Her father's "desertion" couldn't have happened at a worse time. Her mother suffered at least two major depressions; one of them occurred after the birth of her twin sons when Paula was in nursery school. She remembers her mother lying on the couch and tearfully recalled being in nursery school listening for her father's footsteps, signalling his return to get her.

Paula described her mother, one of the youngest in a family of ten children, as having been neglected by her overwhelmed mother and terrorised by a sister who suffered from bipolar disorder. Paula was brought up in a very religious home, in which good and evil were well defined. Her mother was anxious to have all of her children believe as she did; to not do so meant they were going to hell, which would represent her failure as a parent, as well as a separation from her children in the afterlife. Paula's parents worked hard to maintain financial stability, and Paula was quite aware of the sacrifices her mother in particular made to put her through school at a well-known private university.

Paula felt quite ashamed that she experienced periods of intense anxiety as a child. Her mother would treat her impatiently. This, of course, troubled Paula, who both hated to upset her mother and left her feeling quite alone. Listening to her descriptions, it seemed to me that Paula's anxiety stretched her mother's limits quickly, after which she would label Paula a nervous child, adding to an already growing concern Paula had about herself.

Paula often described phone calls with her mother after which, to her surprise, she got off feeling "sour". It was striking that she didn't allow herself to pick up on the very negative, denigrating, and envious messages that came from her mother. Over and over, Paula would report her mother's comments, which always had the effect of undermining any accomplishment or effort Paula was making.

Paula and I explored the idea that men gave up on her easily. As we did so, she began to see that the men she allowed herself to be attracted to were men whom she unconsciously knew were not going to stick around. She was afraid of anyone getting too attached to her because of her unconscious belief that she would have to accommodate them as she had accommodated her mother by tolerating her mother's criticisms and tending to her when she was depressed. She began to be aware that she didn't allow herself to invest fully in relationships, "at most fifty-five to seventy per cent"—a protective measure that characterised all of her relationships.

She began dating an extremely bright man, Frank, who was adoring, patient, and generally unlike her mother. He came from a family in which both education and intelligence were admired, an attitude that stood in contrast to how Paula felt her education and intelligence were viewed, especially by her mother and some of her aunts. While her parents worked hard to provide college educations for her and her siblings, Paula felt that her high intelligence, combined with her move away from her home state, made her mother and other relatives suspicious that she might see herself as better than them.

Paula was quite fascinated by Frank's mother, who enjoyed her children without being possessive. Paula's admiration of Frank's mother was tainted by feelings of guilt for what she deemed as disloyalty to her own mother. Sex was difficult to enjoy with Frank; she had never been really able to feel pleasure in sexual relationships except with the men whom she knew were not available. She feared becoming dependent on Frank, not knowing whether or not he would continue to love her. She also worried that she would become attracted to someone else and betray Frank's trust, which would have been a move designed to counter his growing importance to her.

Paula initially spent a lot of time in her hours describing incidents involving hurtful things people would say and wonder, "Are people being cruel or are they just unaware?" It was a long time before she was able to see her mother's remarks as being hurtful and that her own reaction of feeling "sour" at the end of the phone call made sense. Of course, the issue of whether her mother was deliberately being hurtful came up. After a long time, she finally said, "I never had a mother—she leaves me alone by saying things that indicate she hasn't been pleased." Her dilemma was a painful one: she couldn't please her mother but felt, given how depressed and anxious her mother was, that she was responsible for keeping her alive. This made her continued involvement with her mother essential. She continued her phone calls to her mother, which were tortuous; although her presence on the phone brought out the vigorous, opinionated, and alive mother whom she wanted, she often felt depleted by her mother's opinions, judgements, and questions.

Work in the transference–countertransference helped us to see why she needed to accommodate herself to repetitively negative interactions with her mother. In our hours, Paula seemed eager to see me and discuss the things that bothered her. However, accepting what I had to offer was complicated for her. A pattern developed in which she seemed to resonate with what I said, but then would add another vignette, which agreed with what I had just said, but she said it in a tone that implied she was correcting me a bit. When we discussed this pattern, she stated that she just wanted to make sure I understood the situation and so added another example which I thought signalled some uncertainty on her part. Unconsciously, the message was that my interpretation wasn't quite good enough. This repetitive experience eventually allowed me to understand what she'd had to tolerate with her mother, whom she was never able to please. Her correction of my interpretation ensured that we were never quite in synch. Being in synch and enjoying the relationship aroused anxiety that I was becoming too important to her and signalled that she might then have to comply with what I needed, which she feared would entail re-experiencing the soul-wrenching experience of never being able to please me. This was too big an investment to risk when she often felt like "an orphan waiting to be kicked out".

Paula's fear of being deserted also got played out between us. Often after a "good session", she would miss the next session or two, saying nothing about her absence at the next session she attended unless I brought it up.

Exploration about her absences linked her appreciation of some work we'd done prior to her absence with her fear that she was deserting her mother by being in "another" relationship. She was also unconsciously testing my ability to bring her "disappearance" up in spite of the fact that she ignored it and to inquire about her treating me as if I were unimportant. She had never been able to bring up her mother's depression and the lack of engagement she experienced for fear of further damaging her mother. Her absences were related to not making me too important and expressing some anger about how frightened she was. We could now see that initially her need to stay unaware of the aggression in her mother's responses on the phone kept her safe from the frightening prospect of being overwhelmed by the aggression and losing the tie with her good internalised mother.

Paula had stated, early on in our work, that she wanted to be a mother. When it became clearer that she and Frank were becoming more serious, she felt some hesitation. We continued to explore issues such as: would Frank stay with her; could she have everything she wanted? Would she continue to love him, or become someone like her mother who couldn't appreciate the "gift" of his love? Since the commonly held opinion among the women in her family was that a child ruins the relationship between the parents, would that happen to her and Frank? Was doing something pleasurable tempting the fates? When the issue of whether or not she would be a good mother came up, she found herself imagining that babies are "… like parents", demanding, disappointing, and imprisoning.

Finally, she was ready to try and get pregnant. After some time went by in which she didn't conceive, she consulted a physician. His assessment concluded that she had low ovum reserve and that donor ovum would be needed in order to conceive. Paula was stunned and distraught. It seemed especially unfair after all the hard psychological work she had done to become comfortable in her relationship with Frank, and to want a baby. She found herself thinking again that she would never have much success in life. She returned to feeling that there was something fundamentally wrong with her, her inability to conceive being a concrete representative of that. Guilt and the retribution that could be expected made her think this was punishment for enjoying sex in the past, and for not aligning herself with the religious rules that were so important to her mother. An abortion she had had many years before loomed guiltily in her mind. In addition, the strangeness of the high-tech methods needed to become pregnant represented how far from "home" she was, how separate she was from her mother in particular. Finally, she felt some relief that the baby would not have her genetic makeup, which she had imagined carried some risk of the bipolar disease from which her aunt suffered.

Six months later, Paula was ready to begin her search for a donor. Prior to that, she had spent her time reworking the issues delineated above, along with grieving for the baby she would never have. Her grief showed evidence of being somewhat muted, but she experienced the feelings more deeply and clearly than she could ever remember. The lost baby represented all of the losses she had experienced, losses that were now clearer to her. She realised with surprise that she *had* begun to believe she deserved to get what she wished for.

Throughout this very difficult period, Paula witnessed Frank's grief about her infertility. Seeing how affected he was by her sadness, as well as his regret about not being able to have a child who carried both their genes, touched her deeply and was very reassuring. Not only was there nothing wrong with her in his eyes; she was special.

The decision to use the ovum of a family member immediately appealed to both Frank and Paula. Neither of them wanted to lose the chance to maintain as much of a genetic connection with family as possible. A cousin of Frank's, a young woman of about twenty-three, volunteered to help. Initially, this choice made Paula's mother feel left out and envious, convinced that Paula's choice represented her belief that Frank's family were better and smarter. Paula felt some guilt about her mother's suffering but was not dissuaded from her choice. She also shared her fear of her aunt's bipolar disease with her mother, who having been traumatised by this sister, was mollified, and more willing see Paula's choice as a wise one.

Unfortunately, an ongoing pregnancy has not yet occurred. The second in-vitro cycle produced a brief period of pregnancy, but within a short time Paula miscarried. It was heartbreaking. Paula grieved deeply along with Frank. Seeing his sadness helped alleviate a sense of shame that she felt this so deeply. Sharing her sadness with others, including other women who had miscarried, helped her quiet the familiar thought that she was especially vulnerable to bad things happening in her life. At this point, Paula and Frank plan a third IVF cycle in a few months.

Discussion

Clare had the fantasy of needing to stay "smaller" in relationships. This represented her fear, not that she was less than others, but that her intelligence and charm might cause others to be envious of her and then withdraw their support from her. Acting as if she were less than others was her solution to the dilemma of being special. Staying "small" was an identification with her mother's acting helpless, an attempt to remain a little girl so as not to seem sexual, which she assumed her mother would not want to see, and finally, it kept her away from looking too much like her mother's competitor. Combined, they resulted in a non-existent sex life for Clare.

Both Paula and Clare had experiences with their mothers that affected their ability to form a safe attachment to men and to enjoy life without the need to greatly restrict their psychological freedom and their life choices.

Paula was affected deeply by the loss of an ongoing relationship with her mother for periods of time when she was a preschooler, due to her mother's serious depressions. The losses continued, although at a less severe level, due to her mother's ongoing depression and anxiety. Her exhaustive efforts to keep her mother "alive" through their phone calls illustrated the depth of her need to ignore the aggressive and envious tone of her mother's remarks. At an unconscious level, she feared the acknowledgement would result in her losing contact with her good maternal object, after which she feared she would feel depressed and despairing. She avoided being involved with available men because of the threat that they would abandon her, or that she would betray them. In addition, she was frightened that once in a relationship, she would have to dedicate herself to her partner's needs in the same way she felt she had had to do with her mother. These fears kept her choice of men restricted to those who were unavailable for a committed relationship and a family.

Clare had the fantasy of needing to stay "smaller" in relationships. This represented her fear, not that she was less than others, but that her intelligence and charm might cause others to be envious of her and then withdraw their support from her. Acting as if she were less than others was her solution to the dilemma of being special. Staying "small" was an identification with her mother's acting helpless, an attempt to remain a little girl so as not to seem sexual, which she assumed her mother would not want to see, and finally, it kept her away from looking too much like her mother's competitor. Combined, they resulted in a non-existent sex life for Clare.

The conflicts that had been in place originally for each of these women made their re-appearance as they entered the world of assisted reproduction, where a very intentioned movement towards pregnancy was to be made. Their anxieties about making reliable attachments were once again aroused. However, both Clare and Paula, due to the work they had already done, felt free in a relatively short time to make choices that were signal achievements for both of them and freed them to pursue motherhood. One of the ways this freedom was expressed was in their choice of donor.

Clare's choice to have her donor be an "outsider", not a family member, demonstrated her freedom to choose to be a woman and create her own family privately, with the man of her choice. Paula's decision to have a child was a declaration of independence from the sense of obligation to the needy, critical maternal introject, and her confidence that her less than positive feelings were not toxic.

The emphasis in this chapter was to look at the ways in which each woman's identification with her mother posed serious barriers to being able to form an intimate partnership and become a mother. It should be noted that both of the women in my clinical examples also had considerable strengths, a result of the healthier aspects of their relationships with their mothers. Also, the focus of this chapter was only on the girl's relationship with the mother and did not include the important role the father has on a girl's development.

Psychoanalysis helped both women become aware of the repetition of conflicted relationship patterns and eventually overcome their ambivalence, allowing them to achieve their wish to become mothers. I am not suggesting that psychoanalysis in general, or any particular interpretation cited, would be effective for every woman. The complexity of a person's object relation, defensive positions, as well as ego strengths, would make such a generalisation impossible. The women I discuss had many advantages, including being able to use analysis, and the conflicts and issues discussed in this chapter may not apply to women in different circumstances.

I am also not suggesting that every woman who is ambivalent about motherhood would be better off becoming a mother. The choice to remain childless is not inherently pathological. There are many good reasons people choose to do so.

Case illustrations cannot prove my thesis, or even that psychoanalysis was the cause of the intrapsychic change and resulting resolution of ambivalence that led these women to become mothers. However, as Valliant (1977), Wallerstein (1986), and other life-span developmental researchers have pointed out, when a repeated pattern of self-defeating behaviour, such as becoming involved with unavailable men, persists for five, ten, or even twenty years, and then is resolved during an analysis, it is reasonable to assume that the analysis played some role in these constructive outcomes.

My hope is that this discussion and the experiences of these two women can alert other clinicians to the likelihood of these conflicts in women in their twenties and early thirties, and provide the help they need in order to resolve their ambivalence without having to use assisted reproductive technology.

References

Covington, S. N., & Burns, L. H. (2006). *Infertility Counseling: A Comprehensive Handbook for Clinicians* (2nd edn.) New York: Cambridge University Press.

Hinshelwood, R. (1989). *A Dictionary of Kleinian Thought*. London: Free Association Press.

Mitchell, S. (1988). *Relational Concepts in Psychoanalysis*. Cambridge, MA: Harvard University Press.

Parker, R. (1997). The production and purposes of maternal ambivalence. In: W. Holloway & B. Featherstone (Eds.), *Mothering and Ambivalence*. London: Routledge.

Pines, D. (1990). Pregnancy, miscarriage, and abortion: a psychoanalytic perspective. *The International Journal of Psychoanalysis, 71*: 301–307.

Pines, D. (2012). Identification, desire and transgenerational issues. In: P. Mariotti (Ed.), *The Maternal Lineage*. London: Routledge, Taylor & Frances.

Sandler, J. (1990). On internal object relations. *Journal of the American Psychoanalytic Association, 38*: 859–880.

Valliant, G. (1977). *Adaptation to Life*. Cambridge, MA: Harvard University Press.

Wallerstein, R. (1988). *Forty-Two Lives in Treatment*. New York: Guilford Press.

CHAPTER FOUR

Egg donors and sperm donors: parental identity formation

Mali Mann and Andrea Mann

Infertility is a medical condition that affects many aspects of human life. It affects one's relationship with one's self and consequently influences one's identity as a mother or father. Individuals who resort to assisted reproductive technology (ART) methods experience emotional, physical, social, and financial hardships, which in turn impact their families. How individuals deal with the unexpected emotions depends on personality style, coping mechanisms, and external and familial support systems.

Often, facing infertility and having to deal with its traumatic impact can lead to denial and projection. The traumatic loss of one's ideal self is a challenge for individuals struggling with infertility. One cannot rely upon secondary-process thinking. Unconscious wishes will always be carrying along reason in the course of the decision process and in choosing an egg or sperm donor.

In-vitro fertilisation (IVF) is a process in which an egg is fertilised outside the body. It was first implemented in 1978 and has since increased in use dramatically. Infertility rates have increased over the past several decades, in part due to better forms of contraception, thus decreasing the rate of unplanned pregnancies. A shift towards marrying later in life and a subsequent delay of childbearing also explains higher rates of infertility. Today, one in every eighty to a hundred births in the United States, one in sixty births in Australia, and one in fifty births in Sweden are created through some form of in-vitro fertilisation (IVF) (Van Voorhis, 2007).

Donor eggs

For woman who have circumstances such as premature ovarian failure, advanced age, lower ovarian reserve, autoimmune disease, failed IVF, or concerns about genetically transmitted diseases, donor egg IVF may be considered. Donor eggs can allow a woman to carry a pregnancy to term. Since 2007, around 1,300 women in the United Kingdom every year are treated with donated eggs. There has been a shortage as demand has increased. Some clinics have waiting lists of about one year, which has resulted in many women and couples seeking treatment abroad. Increases in demand have contributed to the growth of the egg market in the United States, where women willing to donate their eggs can earn between $4,000 and $10,000 (Saner, 2012).

Although egg donation is scientifically analogous to artificial insemination with donor sperm, it raises more questions concerning the medical risks and potential psychological impact on the donor, couple, and future child. These factors include expense and medical risk to the woman donating the egg, the risk of the recipient carrying multiple babies to term, as well as ethical and legal issues. Included in the fee for donor eggs is the cost of psychological screening for the donor, genetic counselling, egg donor health insurance for complications, travel fees, and legal fees. This list provides a brief introduction to the complicated nature of selecting and purchasing an egg.

Most egg donors remain anonymous, unless a donor finds a couple willing to engage in an "open egg donation". Psychological issues often appear during the selection process. Couples can browse through egg donor profiles online, much like a dating website. One egg donation company advertises that couples can select an "academic achiever" for an extra $500 (Anonymous, 2011). Some donors and recipient couples need psychological support with the entire egg IVF treatment, donor selection, cycle coordination, egg retrieval, and transfer of embryos.

Although patients have opportunities to explore the concrete details of IVF available in clinician offices or on websites, they often do not explore their own internal fantasy construct. One example of denial of what reality may present is dealing with multiple babies. Unlike their European colleagues, reproductive specialists in the United States tend to transfer multiple embryos at a time, resulting in an increased risk of multiple birth pregnancies. There is potential for both pleasure and peril in carrying multiple babies to term and parenting multiples. Multiple birth pregnancies carry increased risk of premature birth and birth defects. However, providing education before the transfer process could be a pivotal conversation for reproductive physicians and their teams.

During the course of infertility work-up, attention is often focused on external factors (i.e., the medical team) rather than an individual's mind and unconscious fantasy life. These infertility techniques help many women become pregnant, but the interaction between fantasy and reality stimulated by the adult wish for a baby is complicated. Unconscious fantasies are at play before conception, during the pregnancy, and post-partum, and affect transference feelings towards the donor egg, donor sperm, and the child.

A new trend of increased openness and transparency for egg and sperm donors has taken place that follows a similar trend that happened several years ago with adoption. Anonymity and secrecy are becoming outdated. In fact, there are counselling centres that help couples on how best to break the news. There are still some couples who do not dare break the secrecy, due to perceived stigma, fear of forming weaker attachment bonding, and inner conflict. Children of single women and gay and lesbian couples have naturally been curious about their genetic origins. For this reason, these families have initiated this trend of openness about using donors, with some even forming relationships with their child's biological parent. More and more heterosexual parents have also voiced their preference to tell their children how they were conceived—a modern version of the "facts of life" (Ludden, 2011).

When and how to tell a child about his or her biological origins depends on the child's developmental and cognitive capacity to understand the meaning of the information he or she receives. Dishonesty affects a child's sense of trust towards his or her parents. It creates a potential disequilibrium in his or her psychic function and object relations.

Donor sperm

Some men must confront their own infertility issues like their female counterparts. In approximately forty per cent of infertile couples, the male partner is either the sole or a contributing cause of infertility (Nachtigall, 1991). Male infertility may be related to the volume or amount, motility, and morphology of the sperm. A male fertility work-up can involve genetic testing and other hormonal testing. In some cases, no obvious cause of poor sperm quality can be found.

Treatment for male factor infertility may include antibiotic therapy for infection, surgical correction of varicocele (dilated or varicose veins in the scrotum) or duct obstruction, or medications to improve sperm production. In some men, surgery to obtain sperm from the testis can be performed. Intra-uterine insemination (IUI) or in-vitro fertilisation (IVF) may then be recommended.

When male infertility is the cause of the problem, couples have the option to use a sperm donor. Direct injection of a single sperm into an egg, called intra-cytoplasmic sperm injection (ICSI), may be recommended as a part of the IVF process. In men with deformed or absent sperm, the use of this technique can carry some risks. The physician may recommend using a sperm donor. Insemination with donor sperm may also be considered if IUI is not successful or if the couple does not choose to undergo IVF.

Psychologically, men are not immune to feelings of despair and inadequacy when discovering their infertility for the first time. Men might feel infertility as loss of success, as failure, or even a life crisis. Feelings of failure have been associated with feeling in a state of disequilibrium. A chronic, unending sense of fear and anxiety has been described by some men. The recovery from this loss may never reach to a full resolution. The mourning period can linger on for a long time and may become an unfinished mourning. Many men are unable to ask for help to process the intense feelings of disappointment and to recover from the loss. The feeling of "why me?" in particular can erode one's sense of self-confidence as self-doubt sets in.

Cases

Here we describe three cases in psychodynamic psychotherapy that illustrate the complex psychological ramifications of fertility and the impact of ART.

Nelly

Nelly is a thirty-two-year-old married woman who came to psycho-therapy treatment for depression. She was unhappy in her life, suf-fered from poor self-esteem, and harboured ambivalent feelings towards getting pregnant. She had no history of childhood distur-bances and she was accustomed to being an only child. She had a close healthy attachment to her mother. Her developmental milestones were reportedly normal. She had no early memory of any other caregivers besides her mother, although her mother married when she was two years old.

Unconsciously, she identified with her mother, who denigrated her stepfather. Her mother was not a nurturing woman and was often angry with Nelly when she was a young child. In contrast, her stepfather was a caring man who showed affection towards her.

As a child, she was under the impression that she was conceived out of wedlock. After Nelly turned sixteen, her mother told her that she was conceived with the help of a sperm donor. Her mother refused to tell her whether she had used a sperm bank or the sperm from a friend or acquaintance. Her world suddenly became upside down—not knowing anything about her biological origin. Her sense of identity was shaken up. Initially shocked by this tightly kept secret, Nelly became depressed when she could not find out the identity of her biological father. She was angry with her mother who had concealed the truth from her. She developed an obsession with the thought of wanting to find her biologi-cal father.

She needed to know where her chin or nose came from and also why she developed an interest in international relations and cross-cultural psychology. Nelly hoped to forgive her mother for having her out of wedlock, and that someday her mother would tell her about the man by whom she got pregnant. She finally was able to find her father through an Internet search, after much detective work. She wanted to solve the puzzle of "who am I?"

Her mother explained that she was not sure she could marry at age thirty-four and the clock was ticking away. She did not think she could attract a man to marry her. She decided to use an anonymous sperm donor. She told her that her doctor helped her with an anonymous sperm donor. She wanted it to be something like an immaculate con-ception. Nelly's mother, for reasons of her own, did not tell her how she was conceived or where she found the sperm donor. She did not think that far ahead about Nelly's future inquiry into her roots of origin. All Nelly knew was that the man she called Dad was not her biological father. None of her friends knew that Nelly had a stepfather.

Several years later, once Nelly became aware of the intensity of her chronic anger towards her mother, she decided to get psychotherapeutic help. She felt frozen in her life and could not move forward. She was in tears one day, feeling she could not free herself from rage. "I don't understand why my mother did not think about what would happen to me when I had to live in her secret world of lies and deceit! Did she want empathy from me that she was not marriageable and she had to resort to lying to everyone, especially to me? I am a person too!"

After she discovered the biological father, she became angry with him as well. One day, she related, "Now I know who was the donor I am angry with him too. It is like staying anonymous and absolved from his responsibility finished his job! I feel miserable. My mother brought me into this world just to please herself by affirming her feminine and fertile self."

In therapy, she worked on her revived deep sense of shame and narcissistic disappointment. She was ashamed of herself and her mother who lacked self-confidence. She had anxious fantasies that she was joined with her mother eternally and could not find her own autonomous self. She worried her rage would destroy her connection with her mother. Her fear of losing her god-like, childhood image of stepfather mixed with a newly emerging image of this other "father". These fears turned into an anxiety about her identity diffusion. She felt regret for getting herself into "this mess" without knowing how to get out of it. She wondered about repeating what her mother had done. She fantasised about staying childless to get revenge on her mother. She did not want to let technology decide her conception. She struggled with her husband's wish for wanting to have children.

She started to understand her mother's anxiety about her biological clock and uncertainty about her sense of femininity. Nelly became aware of her ambivalent feelings about motherhood and was willing to work through her childhood wish to conceive and bear a child. She learned to value her academic achievement, which was so much greater than her mother's, without having to feel guilty of surpassing her.

Todd

Todd and Sherry are parents of a four-year-old son. Todd presented to therapy because he had difficulty relating to their son, who was conceived by Sherry through sperm donation from a family friend.

In their mid-thirties, after many years of attempting to become pregnant, the couple was evaluated for infertility. Male infertility was identified as the main factor in their difficulty conceiving. Todd recalled the sense of failure when this discovery was made. It was a crisis for him as he cycled through hope, fear, and despair. It was an emotional roller-coaster each time they started a new round of ICSI. After multiple trials, they came to accept the fact that they had to use a donor sperm. He wanted to use his close friend's sperm and his wife agreed to that. When Sherry became pregnant, they were able to go through feelings of anticipation and excitement together as a couple. The pregnancy was uneventful and their healthy baby boy was born. He was a beautiful boy who did not resemble Todd.

He found himself feeling surprised, having noticed some strange feelings towards his infant son and his friend, with whom he had a close friendship and working relationship. In retrospect, he started to have doubts about his decision to use his friend's sperm rather going to a sperm bank. It felt right to ask his good friend at that time, but after Sherry gave birth to their son, he noticed he was having many doubts about his ability to be a good father. How could he have ignored his own longing for a biological relationship with his child? After all, many people went to a cryobank and arranged to get donor sperm. He felt his decision to ask his friend was reasonable at the time. Looking back, he realised his assumption that the "the end product", and not the biological root, was what mattered. He secretly blamed his wife for rushing to get pregnant.

At four years of age, his son looked so much like his friend Peter. He avoided getting together with his friend because he worried his son would show more affinity towards Peter as well as Peter towards him.

He wondered if he could ever have the stamina to keep the secret from his son. He worried that disclosing this to his son would result in him turning away. Should he strip his son from the right to know who his biological father is? He debated with himself whether his son had the right to know that he was not his biological father. How can he and his wife explain all of this to him?

Furthermore, he feared his friend Peter would some day reclaim his right as biological father. He kept wondering what would happen to their marriage when all three of them would attend gatherings, especially when they would also take their son with them. What if Sherry developed a closer connection to Peter and consequently ended their marriage?

The internal dilemma that Todd was facing caused he and his wife much tension. Sherry communicated to him that resorting to sperm donation from his friend was entirely his fault. She reminded him that she had preferred an anonymous donor. They yelled at each other frequently, and argued about many things, especially when it came to decisions about the kind of day care their son was to attend or issues around discipline.

He experienced mixed feelings, especially when recalling Sherry's expectation that he play the role of the supportive husband during her pregnancy. He did not have time to think through his decision and was expected to offer Sherry emotional support. He did not know how to come to terms with his own infertility, let alone to play a new role supporting his wife. He did not know how he could offer support, especially when another man's sperm was involved in this process. The sense of profound failure as a male was a prevailing feeling. He was there for her when she went through the wrenching experience of the harvesting of the ova, but now he felt as if his son was a stranger.

Only in retrospect was he able to think more deeply about the effect that consenting to donor sperm had had on his sense of father identity and paternity rights to their son. He felt tormented with fear that he had in fact a weak bond with his son. He wished he could have foreseen and prevented the psychological complications of his rushed decision.

In his therapy, Todd was able to discuss all of his many fears and self-doubts as non-biological father as well as his role as husband to Sherry. He felt he had to prepare himself to be less emotionally reactive or erratic when he encountered his friend. After all, he could not be ungrateful to his friend, since he was an honourable, altruistic man who had helped to create their son.

He was unprepared for his out-of-control feelings after the baby was born. He agreed to freeze two of Sherry's embryos for future use. He resented the thought of having more kids, fearing having to endure the same familiar range of intense emotions. The emergence of a powerful destructive fantasy was explored during this period of his work with me. How could he deny Sherry from having more babies?

His individual therapy helped him to work through his destructive feelings, manage his intense negative affect, develop a better tolerance, and not act out on them. After much individual work, he became interested in starting couples' therapy. He felt he was in a much better place since he developed a more consolidated sense of himself. He wanted to work towards better stability in his marital relationship.

From post-therapy contact by phone, Todd described feeling that his relationship with his son improved. Although his son did not resemble him physically, he seemd to have the same temperament. He learned the importance of openness, and wanted to tell his son about the sperm donor when he was at a right age to comprehend its meaning. Overall, he was able to enjoy a healthy relationship with him.

Emily

Emily is a married professional in her mid-forties who presented to therapy because of conflict surrounding her marriage and her desire to become a mother. She was doubtful about their capacity to become parents.

She postponed her decision to have a child for many years and suddenly realised time was running fast. Emily was the second child from a family of three children. Her sister was five years older than her and was a very popular girl. She could never be like her sister. She felt her mother preferred her older sister because they both were brunette and had more in common. Emily was blond and petite. The youngest was a girl who was born eight years after Emily's birth. Emily grew up with a pervasive feeling that she was damaged, a feeling that was reinforced by her over-anxious mother throughout her childhood. She was maternal to her younger sister and fiercely competitive to her older sister. Her father drank a lot and used foul language when intoxicated. She learned to avoid him and his abusiveness.

Emily described herself as an obedient girl who never thought of herself as intelligent. Her mother constantly compared her to her older sister, and her father jokingly called her "dumb little blond". She was filled with anxiety and self-doubt. Perpetuating this self-doubt was her family's difficult financial situation, which made her feel inferior to her classmates who were living in comfort.

In her early adolescence, she befriended a girl from a high socio-economic class. She enjoyed her association with her privileged friend, with whom she rode to school in a chauffeured car. She also felt envious of her friend, secretly wishing she could be her. On several occasions, while no one was looking, her friend's grandfather would touch her breasts several times inappropriately. She recalled those early experiences as exciting and at the same time was fraught with shame and guilt. After the friend transferred to another school, Emily had lost contact with that family, including the grandfather. She liked the attention the old man was giving her by having her sit on his lap, but never told anyone.

After completing high school, Emily entered into a prestigious college. She met her husband in college, and after few short months they decided to get married. The couple waited for fifteen years before they decided to start a family.

For several years, Emily was unsuccessful in becoming pregnant. Eventually, they sought gynaecological work-up for infertility, which revealed multiple calcified fibromyoma in her uterus. Her mother also suffered from the same problem. However, her mother had her three children before her fibromyoma became problematic. Emily's contributing psychological makeup complicated her infertility problem further.

Her difficulty conceiving made Emily feel as though she was "damaged goods". She could not become a mother like her sister, or even her own mother. She was bitter and could not accept that her uterine abnormality was the cause of her infertility. She felt it was not fair that her sister had children and she could not get pregnant. She was a "virtuous good girl" and her mother relied on her when her family needed help. She felt she was denied something very important. "It was my birth right, it was not fair!", she said one day, trying to draw affirmation from me.

On the other hand, after she found out she could not conceive, she thought "there was a big sign on me like in Scarlet letters that I was infertile". The fertility clinic told her she needed to talk to a psychiatrist because her infertility was "psychogenic". Later, she reported, "I was going to a full circle. I thought I was grieving. I was so disappointed each time I tried. My husband was not grieving. But, to be fair to him, he actually was very supportive of me and left me free to make a decision how to go forward. He even was willing to be childless if I wanted to."

In one of her analytical hours, she said "I must have made myself infertile by being neurotic. See, I am not smart to catch on to things quickly. See, pregnancy may never happen for me. Maybe I wanted it too much, like I wanted my friend's wealth and prestige. I wanted to wear expensive clothes, drive an expensive car, and marry a rich man. It may be wanting everything or wanting too much, being greedy has to do with not getting what I really want, a family is what I have always dreamt of." She had tears in her eyes. She was in despair and full of doubt. She continued, "I did not even ask why I needed to talk to a psychiatrist. I followed their advice. Looking back, I could tell why I needed to see someone, and now I am here to see you in order to understand my ambivalent feelings about motherhood."

She felt she needed me to help her learn to accept her fate, or maybe she would regain her stamina to pursue other options such as using an egg donor, or resign to the prospect of being childless. She had contemplated using a surrogate mother, but wanted to try the egg donor option with her newly reconstructed uterus. (She had gone through extensive myomectomy.) Her two IVFs and GIFT (gamete in the Fallopian tube) procedures were unsuccessful. These failures caused her great anguish, hopelessness, and self-doubt.

She realised how angry she was with her mother, who did not empower her and instead made her a damaged woman. She also felt that I was an impotent analyst and that her problem was far more complicated, beyond the scope of my expertise to be able to solve. She was unsure about the help I could offer her. In the transference, I turned into an "infertile analyst". She agreed with my interpretation of how she wished I could have had a magic formula to help her damaged uterus, damaged mind, and damaged body. She felt I was letting her suffer in her despair and was being indifferent to her pain. I emerged as a controlling pre-oedipal mother who expected total obedience and submission.

The decision about using an egg donor and who to ask became an obsession that agonised her for many months. She thought about asking her younger sister to become her egg donor. She asked herself if her sister would have second thoughts about going through the medical procedure. She wanted her child to have her family genes and not to go to a stranger for eggs.

After several months of deliberation, she got her courage up to ask her sister Ann to see if she was willing to be her donor. Ann was a mother of two and was happily married. She was eager to help her older sister, of whom she was very fond. Emily was ecstatic when she heard her sister accepted to be her egg donor. We tried to explore the meaning of using the eggs from her sister.

Her desire to use her sister's eggs was so strong that she was not interested to explore the meaning of her decision. Her conscious desire was to have her family genes pull with her husband's sperm, rather than using eggs from some stranger whom she did not know. She was set to have her own child, and if her sister was willing to give her eggs, it meant that those were like her own eggs. "It's like a dress we could both share" was how she described it, with glee on her face. Shortly after this decision, she started to have fears about her sister's children, who would be her child's half-siblings. How could she bear the thought of keeping it secret, or bear to have it out in the open?

One happy thought countering her fear was "why not become a big happy family?" She would carry the baby to term and everyone would understand and support her. She also thought she was being greedy to ask for her sister's eggs, which were not hers. To her, it was like stealing. This self-accusation led to an association to an earlier memory about her mother. She recalled how her mother declared one day how could she feed her children when there was hardy any food at home. Her father, an alcoholic, was not helping the family when he spent money on his alcohol. Food was scarce, and the family had to deal with extreme deprivation.

Over time, our analytical work helped her with feelings of envy, greediness, and stealing. She worked hard to overcome her doubt and move forward with her decision to enter into the world of motherhood.

After this unsettling emotional period, she became more hopeful as she anticipated becoming a mother. Emily overcame her disabling doubts. Her pregnancy was uneventful and she gave birth to a healthy baby girl. She brought her baby infant to one of her sessions. The baby had resemblance to her. She wanted to hear my reassurance that indeed her daughter looked like her. It was very important to her to hear it from me.

Two years later, after a period of hiatus in her treatment, she phoned to see me for a follow-up visit. She was caught by surprise when she began feeling confused about her reaction towards her sister on a holiday family gathering. She felt her daughter seemed to go to her aunt (her biological mother), and she imagined her sister also made obvious her attraction to her daughter through her non-verbal interaction. She told me that she had never thought about how she might feel about her future encounters within her family circle or her potential unexpected emotional reaction. She knew her sister had not revealed to her own two children about having volunteered to be an egg donor to her older sister. Emily was not prepared to talk about it with her daughter and was not sure that she would have wanted to disclose to her.

Although she did not continue therapy, she would have benefited by exploring the meaning of her belief in "the promise of anonymity". She felt competitive towards her sister and felt inferior to her. She continued to struggle with her reawakened old feelings about her body that had betrayed her.

Discussion

Each of these cases contains many complex elements—social, familial, and cultural, as well as unconscious and conscious components. These aspects influence the way in which individuals navigate infertility through unexpected challenges and losses.

For some men, infertility is often experienced as performance failure—a failure of masculinity. Others may not experience it as directly affecting their traditional gender role, despite feeling profoundly disappointed. In some cultures, masculinity and femininity are directly linked to being able to produce children. Female fertility is a very public experience, displayed by visible bodily changes. There is no parallel public display of fertility and sexuality for men. Furthermore, bearing children is often a rite of passage for women; closely tied to their sense of femininity and role in society. In cultures that value women primarily for their ability to produce children, infertility or menopause marks a shift away from a position of prominence.

For both men and women, infertility can cause physical and emotional turmoil—which has unique and complex dimensions for every couple. Although ART has helped produce many successful pregnancies, the emotional impact of these reproductive methods requires further examination. The invasive aspect of the medical work-up (i.e., gynaecological exam, intravaginal ultrasound, etc.), followed by medical interventions (i.e., oral medications, injectable hormones, surgical sampling of sperm), before a successful pregnancy, can be extremely stressful, and can psychologically unravel the individual and shake up even the healthiest couple. It can be a private and lonely experience for couples when social support is limited.

On a more existential level, infertility affects individuals' sense of who they are and who they imagined they would become. The fundamental value—a capacity for creation—has been so deeply rooted in a sense of bodily self that belief systems about one's identity become challenged. Patients struggle consciously and unconsciously with the meaning of borrowing eggs or sperm from other people. Earlier unconscious conflicts reappear and affect their sense of identity and their relationship as a couple. Intense emotions erupt without people knowing how to manage them while they are undergoing reproductive procedures, and even several years later as parents of an ART child. Analysts and psychotherapists can offer a safe holding environment in which to explore these thoughts and emotions.

References

Anonymous (2011). *Parents' Frequently Asked Questions*. Retrieved from http://www.bhed.com/become-parent-egg-donor-program.php.

Ludden, J. (2011). A new openness for donor kids about their biology. NPR: Making Babies: 21st Century Families. Retrieved from http://www.npr.org/2011/09/17/140476716/a-new-openness-for-donor-kids-about-their-biology (17 September).

Nachtigall, R., & Mehren, E. (1991). *Overcoming Infertility: A Practical Strategy for Navigating the Emotional, Medical, and Financial Minefields of Trying to Have a Baby*. New York: Doubleday.

Saner, E. (2012). I think of my egg donor every day. *The Guardian*. Retrieved from http://www.theguardian.com/society/2012/dec/13/egg-donation-donor-recipient-experience (12 December).

Van Voorhis, B. J. (2007). In-vitro fertilization. *New England Journal of Medicine, 356*: 379–386.

CHAPTER FIVE

Infertility, trauma, and assisted reproductive technology: psychoanalytic perspectives

Monisha Nayar-Akhtar

Psychoanalysis has long had a complex and psychologically nuanced relationship with infertility and with the treatment of women suffering from infertility. From once being seen as the treatment of choice for women suffering from infertility, it is now the least sought-after psychological intervention for infertility (Apfel & Keylor, 2002; Downey, 1991). This decline warrants further attention and examination.

In an extensive review of the psychoanalytic literature, Apfel and Keylor (2002) suggest that for many years, the primary psychoanalytic focus has been on "psychogenic explanations", with an emphasis on "unconscious repudiation of femininity and motherhood, and fears of sexuality". This focus has become increasingly more problematic, obsolete, and outdated, as cultural and social factors altering the reproductive trajectories for women (as many women postpone starting their families or choose same-sex partners), suggest that infertility and/or the use of assisted reproductive technologies can now result from exercising personal choice and occur as a result of delay in choosing when to have a child. In addition, the mushrooming of several goal-focused brief psychotherapy options has provided the lure of quickly moving through and resolving (superficially) any and all psychological issues related to the current biological predicament of infertility. This trend was noted almost twenty years ago by Leon (1996), who wrote: "adherence to certain unproven psychoanalytic beliefs in the area of reproductive psychology as well as overlooking the benefits of less intensive, psychoanalytically informed short-term approaches may obstruct psychoanalytic contributions in this area" (p. 342). These observations are significant and point to an imperative need to understand infertility, assisted reproductive technology, and the suffering of women in a more nuanced way.

It is widely acknowledged that narratives of infertility are quite complex, and it remains a deeply emotional experience for all couples affected by it. At its core, it remains a private and lonely experience for a woman who is unable to bear a child at any age. Compounded by personal, social, familial, and cultural narratives, each woman's experience has conscious and unconscious elements that inform her decisions and help her navigate the developmental trajectory of her adult life with inherent losses that are implied in this procedure. Apfel and Keylor (2002) capture this succinctly when they write

> psychological conflicts involving infertility reach into the deepest layers of the individual psyche, invade the interpersonal space of the couple and radiate into the cultural surround and its definition of family. Old conflicts are frequently revived which may challenge the integrity of the marital relationship. A couple's pain is then compounded beyond their involuntary childlessness by invasive procedures and ethical dilemmas created by recent technological opportunities. (p. 86)

Psychological impact of assisted reproductive technology

Contemporary contributions to the understanding of infertility suggest that the psychological treatment of this biological situation would be more nuanced. Certainly, advances in medical technology regarding the act of conception and the physical bearing of a child have altered and shaped the nature of interpersonal relationships, offering women and couples choices as to when and how to have a child. Today, assisted reproductive technology (from donor eggs to in-vitro fertilisation to the phenomenon of frozen eggs) offer a plethora of choices to women who either voluntarily or involuntarily postpone the act of bearing a child. Regardless of how a woman arrives at her decision, the procedure is complicated, lengthy, time-consuming, emotionally exhaustive, and financially exorbitant. No one leaves this treatment without a multitude of feelings regarding the interventions, the manner of delivery, the lack of suitable mourning when something goes awry (Gentile, 2013), and guilt for what they perceive as failure on the part of their bodies to do what they once thought they could and should do.

Psychoanalysts described a wide range of psychological factors to account for the infertility. These ranged from

> unconscious fears and conflicts over sex and pregnancy, rejection of feminine/maternal identification and one's reproductive destiny, rivalry and ensuring guilt toward male family members, wishes to remain dependent, identification with the father, envy of masculinity, guilt and hostility toward a disabled and/or deceased male sibling and insecure or disorganized primary attachment. (Apfel & Keylor, 2002)

Conflicts and ambivalence surrounding maternal identifications was seen as central to cases of infertility by Chodorow (2003), who described "constellations of unconscious mother–daughter–daughter sibling fantasies, anchored by a deadened aggression against both self and object, that destabilised and undermined fertility and maternality" (p. 1181). Contemporary advances in psychoanalytic thinking framed these issues within a cultural and interpersonal context (Rosen & Rosen, 2007) by elaborating further on the, often unconscious, conceptions of gender and sexuality that impact decisions about when and how to bear a child.

Strikingly absent in the literature are reports of women who, after having conceived a child through assisted reproduction technology, seek treatment for psychological issues. Very little is noted about their concerns about motherhood, and the few reports that are available suggest a denial of any negative feelings regarding their status as a mother (Chodorow, 2003; Jaffe & Diamond, 2005). The development of one's notion of motherhood and how one participates in and experiences this role emerges as a significant and powerful variable in the psychological constellation. Recognising that while emotional sequalae to one's decision to postpone having a child may be complicated, the actual choice itself is liberating regardless of the context within which it appears, Chodorow (1999, p. 16) draws attention to cultural trends to describe "pregnancy and childbirth", and describes the "felt reproductive drive (as being) filtered through the prism of the intrapsychic and intersubjective reproduction of mothering" (p. 1183). Motherhood is a complex emotional state and certain experiences are central to the emergence of this internal construct. Central to the development of a woman's psychosexual self and object-relational self, psychoanalysts have explored it as an adult developmental phase or even one that results from a psychosocial crisis (Balsam, 1996; Bibring, 1959; Chodorow, 1978). According to Chodorow (2003), "any woman's desire for children whether immediately fulfilled, fulfilled belatedly, or never fulfilled, contains layers of affect and meaning" (p. 1184). The recognition that motherhood is a complex construct, and the investigation of infertility versus the treatment of its delay with conscious choice, challenges the notion of "psychogenic infertility" and suggests that it would behoove us to expand our conceptual horizon at this time.

The conscious decision to delay having a child and the subsequent complications in infertility that often arise for women led to the term "reproductive story" coined by Jaffe and Diamond (2005), which captures "the patients' hopes and dreams about having a family, the visions of what their children will be like, as well as how they will parent, them ... at times conscious but largely unconscious narrative, that they create about parenthood" (p. 10). The reproductive story is an integral part of an adult identity and part of their personal self-narrative. The reproductive story begins early in early childhood and it evolves over time. It is a "developmental theory that reaches into one's unconscious dreams, is affected by cultural and social mores, and becomes an integral part of the sense of self" (Jaffe & Diamond, 2005). As such, it is strongly influenced by how one is parented and the messages that one receives about parenting. Family history and early trauma can impact the reproductive narrative such as "family constellation, cultural narratives and norms, family history, history of trauma, family love, ethnic and religious background, peer group norms, media role and the impact of medical technology" (Jaffe & Diamond, 2005).

Jaffe and Diamond (2005) elaborate on a woman's experience of the chronic nature of infertility, the numerous losses that are endured, the intrusive nature of medical procedures, and the impact this has on her emotional state. Acknowledging a failed "reproductive story" is an inevitable part of treatment when a woman seeks psychological help for infertility as she is also undergoing medical procedures. But what of those women who have been the recipients of assisted reproductive technology, have raised their children, and are experiencing emotional difficulties later in life? Do their reproductive stories and reproductive traumas have little or no bearing on the experience of psychological distress? Or is the picture more complex and nuanced and one that emerges during the course of in-depth work informed by their personal histories and narratives of choice.

Some recent attempts to shed light on this can be seen in contemporary psychoanalytic theorising about infertility. They have focused on two significant dynamics: (a) failure to adequately mourn a previous loss; and (b) the absence of ambivalence and disavowal of negative feelings about pregnancy and motherhood that is frequently seen in infertile women (Apfel & Keylor, 2002). Review of the literature reveals a significant correlation between infertility and early separation from parent and unmourned parental death (Christie, 1997), though a failure to mourn the loss of a sibling or defectiveness of a male sibling has also been correlated with cases of infertility (Allison, 1997).

Elaborating on the second dynamic, Kemeter and Fiegl (1998) believe that a desperate need to control and deny ambivalent feelings leads to a repression of negative thoughts and feelings. This in turn has a physiological suppressing impact on fertility. Women who demonstrate these dynamics often find earlier separation–individuation conflicts reactivated. This threatens their already fragile sense of self and leads to the formation of rigid defences and coping styles.

The relationship between trauma and assisted reproductive technology

Exploring socio-cultural and familial experiences that impact on a women's decision to delay having a child undoubtedly broadens the therapeutic landscape for those who treatment infertility. But it does not end there. For anyone working with women, couples, and families, these theoretical trends, along with advances in the treatment of trauma and attachment disorders, clearly suggest that the picture for the contemporary woman and her clinician can be quite complex. While some have attempted to investigate the relationship between premorbid factors and infertility (Vartiainen et al., 1994), the findings have been largely inconclusive. Moreover, there is little that has been reported on the psychoanalytic treatment of women, later in life, who entered motherhood through the use of assisted reproductive technology.

That is not to say that the procedure of assisted reproductive technology in itself is not experienced as being traumatic for the individual and family that find themselves in this situation. With its numerous medical interventions, the sterile environment in which this emotionally loaded biological transaction is conducted, and the cavalier attitude of the supportive staff when things go awry, assisted reproduction and its entourage of players remains a complex, intriguing, and at times disturbing, phenomenon. Given the impersonal atmosphere of the process itself, women who have gone through assisted reproductive technology to conceive a child would bear the emotional vicissitudes of this experience. In conjunction with prior histories of unmourned loss (parent, sibling, and others) and a complex trajectory of ambivalent feelings towards self and other, one can hypothesise that their relationship with their offspring would be profoundly complex. It is with this in mind that this chapter is written. Drawing upon my work with Ms J and Ms M, I will explore the complex relationship that exists between narratives of trauma, infertility, and the long-term impact on psychological functioning.

Ms J

Ms J and I have been working for over ten years. Prior to her work with me, Ms J sought treatment from two doctors. Each treatment was psychoanalytically informed and extensive. However, her symptoms of despair, depression, severe social anxiety, inability to function, and social isolation did not diminish. Upon reaching an impasse in her last treatment that had lasted eight years, Ms J decided to leave. She was referred to me and we began our work, meeting five times a week.

Ms J's transferential relationship with me evolved under a cloud of nervous anxiety and despair (especially when I left town). Feeling abandoned, she would become increasingly demanding and punitive, insisting that I not leave, instilling guilt, threatening to hurt herself, and eventually resorting to crying and pleading. After our initial work stabilised some of these behaviours, Ms J turned to Googling me to learn about what conference I might be attending and where I might be vacationing. Her initial reactions to any knowledge gained from her Internet access (particularly when she acquired information on personal matters) were despair, sorrow, anger, rage, and feelings of inadequacy. Eventually, she would resort to pleas that I love her and not abandon her in any way. We weathered these storms, making gradual strides in our understanding and containment of her tumultuous affects. While our work together undoubtedly contributed to her increasing insight, I was also aware of Ms J's deep attachment to her only son (who was nine years old when we began our work and was conceived through the use of assisted reproductive technology, when she was in her mid-forties). This often provided the external scaffolding to contain her affective states, especially when Ms J felt suicidal and on the brink of emotional collapse. As she sometimes would say, "I cannot leave him alone, I cannot commit suicide as he is everything to me, I conceived him with such difficulty, and I must stay around and I cannot leave." Ms J had conceived her only child through the use of reproductive technology though it had not been easy. This aspect of her adult life trajectory became more apparent as our work progressed, and we could delve deeper into the underlying psychological issues that informed her decision to postpone having her child.

Ms M

In a similar vein, my work with Ms M, an eighty-year-old social worker, examined and explored many aspects of her adult life. She was referred to me for depression, though upon my first meeting, I became immediately aware of seething rage that simmered just below her rather severe and sombre countenance. She was angry with her husband and her children, primarily her daughter, and complained of having few friends, of not having had the life she wanted and, as she was nearing the end of her life, wondered what she had really achieved. Her depression accompanied her like a dark cloud wherever she went, and over the years she had become increasingly isolated, alienated from her social circle and her family, unhappy in her marriage, and resentful of her several family obligations. Her sour and dour mood was clearly evident early on in our work, and it was only towards the end of our work when her reproductive history became available, along with "dark secrets" surrounding the conception of her three children, that Ms M could attain a sense of internal peace and stability that she had hitherto lacked.

Both Ms J and Ms M presented with complex reproductive histories, though the dynamics surrounding this did not become evident till much later in our work. They were both the recipients of assisted reproductive technology, at different times, as they were a generation apart in age. Their emotionally tinged reproductive decisions were undoubtedly shaped by the prevailing medical climate as well as by their personal histories of trauma and choice. While it is true that the practice of assisted reproductive technology has come a long way, so to speak, with unlimited access to knowledge and enhanced decision-making, the emotional sequalae of this medical intervention have not diminished. The gradually increasing body of literature on this subject attests to the delicate balance that now exists for women who choose this procedure in light of the well-known trajectories of medical interventions gone awry and the potential space for physical and emotional assault that exists when one chooses to go down this route. Drawing upon the psychoanalytic treatment of Ms J and Ms M, I hope to explore the complex psychological issues that emerge, and the powerful and poignant meanings that their choices about conceiving their children have had on their lives.

Working with Ms J

Ms J lived in a suburban neighbourhood of a large city, having relocated several years ago when she married her husband in her early forties. Prior to that, Ms J enjoyed a life of relative solitude in a bustling large city, where she maintained a small group of friends, became of a patron of the arts, and occasionally dated, with encouragement from her psychiatrist. Ms J's stunted sexual history had been explored in her therapy, though little could be understood of her inability to feel comfortable sexually and emotionally with her current partners. With time, however, Ms J became concerned about her biological clock and finally married someone, more out of necessity and her deep desire to have a biological child. She was in her mid-forties when she conceived her only son.

The early years of our analytic work were directed towards the containment and analytic exploration of her overwhelming affects and behaviours, and to the gradual reconstruction of her early childhood that could help us understand her abject sense of loss and despair when she, as she put it, "felt un-tethered by me". Rarely did Ms J mention her son or her husband, a man who in this second marriage brought two young children along with him. Though Ms J occasionally alluded to the difficulties of being a stepmother, she rarely explored this further in therapy. In fact, she actively resisted gentle nudging on my part, complaining and admonishing me in my gestures as she felt that this took time "away from her needs, wishes and desires and that her treatment was entirely for her". Interestingly, she remained committed to her role of being a mother, sacrificing her personal professional goals to remain home with her son. She participated in several groups that helped inform her of how to raise her young son, beginning the day he was born.

Her mind having been totally preoccupied with the wellbeing of her son did not, however, become part of the analytic discourse till much later in our work. Quietly, I noted her omissions but remained silent. Gradually, through her associations, working through dreams, and my probing, more conscious descriptions of her pregnancy and associated complications began to appear. As the treatment deepened, Ms J spoke of her "frozen eggs", now housed in the medical centre that had once helped her to conceive her only child. But these associations often appeared in the context of idealising and erotic homosexual feelings towards me. Probing into such associations initially led to Ms J's fantasy of being held by me, much like a mother. Her wish to be close to me was tinged with both desire and repulsion, as she feared the feelings of merging with me as much as she desired being close to me. Gradually, envy of my motherly status emerged (having learned while Googling me that I was the mother of two daughters). She wished to have more children and had dutifully preserved her frozen eggs for several years. We explored the possibility of her bearing another child (recognising the myriad of meanings behind these wishes). As Ms J struggled with these issues, a practical concern involving the eggs arose. Ms J could not hold on to them indefinitely. The frozen eggs involved her husband's sperm and a donor egg, and Ms J was aware of the fact that she was growing older and that carrying a foetus to a full-term pregnancy would remain unavailable as an option. In addition, Ms J was beginning to blossom during the course of our work, branching out professionally, personally, and emotionally. Her increased participation in and enjoyment of new experiences also made the decision of bearing another child more complicated and conflicted.

Seizing such moments, I would inquire about her reproductive history and story. Gradually, a more complicated psychological and biological history emerged. Ms J's adult sexual history was rather sparse, and she had her first sexual experience in her mid-thirties. The reasons for this were complex. Ms J had grown up in a wealthy Mid-Western family, with three sisters and four brothers. Her early childhood memories were of her parents travelling extensively and leaving her in the care of different, predominantly African American, nannies. Her mother was a beautiful woman who often displayed a dark side to her nature when she found herself overwhelmed with the responsibilities of taking care of her young children. She was not a particularly warm or comforting person, and Ms J recalled few memories of feeling close to her mother. Both parents were described as sexually stimulating, as parental nudity was not uncommon, as were frequent references to sexual material, sexual innuendoes, and inappropriate sexual conduct. Ms J's troubled childhood years, accompanied by the history of loss and abandonment, led to her stunted emotional/sexual development during adolescence. Her attempts to seek and establish a safe identity for herself led to frequent school transfers accompanied by a plethora of complicated losses and anxieties. Meanwhile, the family became increasingly fragmented and her parents divorced when she was in her twenties.

Her adolescent years were marked with a history of anorexia, with self-mutilation and a painful absence of any sexual contact or imagination. Ms J's stunted sexual development continued well into her thirties, and it was during her first lengthy treatment that she, upon encouragement from her psychiatrist, engaged in a sexual experience for the first time. Eventually, she married, guided by a strong desire to have a child, several children if she could. Ms J's advanced age for conception placed her automatically at risk for bearing a child, and she found it rather difficult to get pregnant. Medical exploration revealed genetic difficulties in conceiving a child, and the couple sought advanced medical technology to help with the dilemma of getting pregnant.

After several painful procedures accompanied by losses and complications, Ms J conceived her one and only child. Wishing to keep her options to have more children open, she froze her eggs as well as donor eggs, which remain housed in the medical facility she used. Ms J has been unable to let go of these eggs despite the fact that it has been over ten years and she is no longer able or willing to bear a child.

As our work deepened, Ms J's deep love for her only son translated into fears that she would somehow lose him, especially as he grew older and his range of activities increased to include driving, going out with friends, surfing the Internet, and engaging in possibly drinking and driving. Her obsessive fears would often leave her paralysed and unable to function. She projected her feelings onto her son and saw him being flooded with overwhelming affects and anxieties, especially those related to sexuality. Death of her son was an inevitable outcome and this was a palpable unbearable loss.

We continued to explore her anxieties and deepest fears, moving to and fro from her genetic history to current realities. Working through these sometimes overlapping concerns, Ms J began to explore the delicate nature of her pregnancies, including the numerous losses and the sterile medical intrusions that often left her bereft and quite alone. While this resonated with many of her childhood experiences, Ms J could now understand how her emotional state often clouded her judgement, especially regarding her son's ability to choose wisely for himself. She could not envision him as a separate entity, and her inability to do so often resulted in attributing to him motivations and desires that during her adolescent years had left her devastated. She feared losing him just as she had indeed experienced and lived through losing herself. But the difficulty with which she conceived him, as she put it, compounded her whole experience and left her feeling helpless and cheated of her "reproductive story".

Working with Ms M

Depression and anxiety were the salient features of Ms M's presenting complaints. She had a long-standing history of depression, and her sour and dour mood were amply evidenced in her sombre and stern facial features. Rarely did she smile, and her downturned lips and sad dark eyes conveyed a lifetime of agony and despair.

Ms M was a retired mental health worker. After having raised her own family of three children, the oldest of whom was a girl, she now lived with her husband of over fifty-five years. The couple lived in a modest suburban home and saw their children occasionally for family gatherings and religious holidays. Ms M's depression appeared chronic in nature as she complained of having had similar symptoms all her life. She had never sought any treatment, feeling that it would draw attention to her ineptitude as a mental health worker, and she feared criticism and ridicule. Gradually, as our work progressed, a more complex family history emerged.

Ms M had raised her three children while continuing to work. Relying on babysitters and occasional family help, she described herself as being a stern, uncompromising, and unrelenting mother who often set harsh rules and lived by them unflinchingly. Her two sons, both professionals and established in their careers, gave her little difficulty, and her relationship with them continued without significant complications. However, her relationship with her only daughter was significantly marred from childhood. She described her daughter as being strong-willed, and prone to physical violence and verbal abuse. She recalled how as a young girl of eight years, she threw a "fit" (which involved tearing up her favourite party dress that she had received as a gift) when asked to put her away the toys she had received for her birthday. Her daughter's uncontrollable rage directed at her parents, particularly her mother, became a family preoccupation, with both brothers gradually growing to resent their sister. Her daughter's teenage years were marked with increasing physical and verbal abuse, especially towards Ms M. Needless to say, with time, as they grew older, the siblings and the family grew apart. At the time she contacted me, Ms M reported few family gatherings. This was a source of great distress and anguish for Ms M and this was evident to me from the start of our work together. As our work deepened, Ms M voiced her deepest desire to have a better relationship with her daughter and her grandchildren. However, it was several years into our work before Ms M's fantasies of what went awry could be understood and explored.

Ms M struggled to understand her daughter; her oldest child conceived when she was in her late twenties. She took her to several therapists who recommended a variety of treatments, from drugs to behaviour management to even institutionalising her for a period of time. Ms M could not bring herself to put her "daughter away" and coped the best she could. Gradually, a more complicated picture of anger, resentment, and guilt emerged. Her husband, she informed me, was virtually absent as a father. A quiet, gentle, and retiring man who preferred the company of books to that of his children, he would retreat and bury himself in his library. Ms M found him to be a poor and silent partner. Over time, this added to her fury and discontent in the marriage. Though she had often contemplated divorce and felt that she would have been better off without him, she never did leave. They had now been married for over fifty years, and despite her litany of complaints, she now found herself worrying about his failing health and thoughts of an impending loss.

It was clear that Ms M had a complicated life story, and I wondered whether a thread of such discontent and anguish might have been present earlier as well. As her narrative unfolded, I learned the following.

Ms M grew up the oldest of three children. Her parents, of European-Judaeo descent, immigrated to the United States when she was three years old. Her earliest memory of landing in the new country was fraught with fear and anxiety as she remembered being unable to say her name when asked by the intimating US officer upon her arrival at Ellis Island. Her stunned silence and muted response characterised much of her later development as she spent much of her time pursuing her studies or, as she put it, hiding under the bed, mewing when experiencing agonising pain. Often, this emerged when she felt overwhelmed with longings. One memory in particular centred on her longing for a favourite aunt to notice her and include her in her life. She missed her aunt tremendously when her aunt left to return to her home state but she could never voice her feelings to anyone.

Ms M's immigrant parents attempted to assimilate and adjust to their new life quickly, with her mother becoming a seamstress of some repute and her father setting up a junk business. While their vocations were financially lucrative for their family, and they could afford and pursue their moderate needs and desires, it also, as I eventually learned, became a source of shame and guilt. Ms M was acutely aware of her father's business and her reluctance to bring friends home as the front and back yards were strewn with junk that he bartered and dealt with in his daily business. The ensuing shame was further complicated as Ms M became the only beneficiary of her family's relative wealth. Her parents financed her college education, which allowed Ms M to pursue mental health training. However, her siblings were never offered this financial support and were therefore unable to attend college. Ms M was painfully aware of this discrimination along with her parents' vocational choices and immigration status. It set her apart from her siblings, induced feelings of gratitude and shame, and in the end, complicated her adult life as she sought more for herself, only to find herself a victim of her past.

In college, Ms M pursued a career in mental health counselling and, meanwhile, began dating to find herself a husband. Soon, she met her current husband, a dashing and handsome young man who wooed her with his dancing and twinkling blue eyes. Within a year, the two were married, but it was only several years later that they agreed to start a family. Ms M had her daughter and within a matter of six years had her three children. Ms M continued to work as a counsellor in a school district for many years and eventually retired in her mid-sixties. It was only towards the end of our work, which spanned five years, did I learn about how she had conceived her children.

As our work deepened, Ms M's anguish, pain, and sorrow with her daughter became more palpable. I drew her attention to her stern and uncompromising attitude and asked her to tell me more about herself. Ms M described her young adult life with her children as existing between two homes. They had family dinners with her father and mother every Sunday and the children were expected to behave a certain way. After her mother died, Ms M assumed the responsibility of caretaking for her father. Her two younger sisters held minimum-paying jobs and Ms M's guilt over her privileged educational background, paid for by her parents, often prevented her from demanding more help from her sisters. Her middle sister eventually married and moved out of state, and she had died of cancer some ten years ago. She had married a physician and led a comfortable life, unlike that of Ms M, whose marital and family life was constantly filled with strife and anger. Her younger sister also moved away but never married. She worked in an educational institution as an administrative assistant until she retired. Later, a diagnosis of Alzheimer's led to her return to her home state, and she now lived in an assisted living facility with Ms M as her guardian. As the only surviving member of her family of origin, Ms M felt extremely alone, angry, and anxious, wondering if she was next in line for either cancer or Alzheimer's. Ms M's feelings of "survivor guilt" could now be seen in an expanded context.

Explorations in our work led to eventual changes in her personal life. She began to contact her daughter and spend time with her and her grandchildren. Her complaints about them lessened as her depression began to lift. Encouraged by glimpses of her rather dry sense of humour and her ability to banter with me during her sessions, I commented on how I saw an aspect of her that was fun-loving and gregarious. Ms M then revealed how she was drawn to her husband and fell in love with him because "he was a dashing dancer". I listened quietly as she began to draw me more into her personal world of marital life. It was then that I learned of how, when she was unable to conceive a child with her husband, she had sought the help of a local doctor. He recommended an anonymous sperm donor (as was customary in those days), and she pursued this with all her three children, each conceived with a help of a stranger. The secret of her children's conception was only known to her and to her husband. Her children only knew the father who raised them. They had no knowledge of the sperm donors. And now, I was placed in a mix of silence.

Ms M's revelation to me added another dimension to our work, but one that could not be explored fully as I was closing down my practice for personal reasons. Several months prior to my gaining knowledge of her reproductive history, I had informed her that I was moving out of state. I pondered about Ms M's unconscious motivations for sharing the concrete details of her reproductive story with me almost near the end of our work. Though time did not permit us to delve into this deeper, I have often wondered about its long-term impact on me as I find myself returning to this over and over again (having presented this enactment, which was never analysed, in several different venues). I decided to bear this revelation in silence and allow Ms M the relief she needed at that time. In the remaining time, we explored her profound guilt, shame, and anger and sadness that she now felt when she saw her children. She wondered who their biological fathers could be, whether they lived in the area. She had no way to contact the doctor who had worked with her as he had long passed away. I was struck by how now, I, too, in moving away, would have no knowledge of Ms M, and in the space of our mutual yet at times discordant silence, wondered if we could find a way to connect. I marvelled at how Ms M had remained silent all these years, much like the girl who immigrated and become mute. Some sorrows are borne in silence, and it is in the unearthing of a narrative that one heals.

Discussion

The medical practice of assisted reproductive technology provides women the option of postponing their childbearing years, affording them the assurance that they can and will bear a child even when their bodies resist and do not comply with their expectations. Nevertheless, the road travelled by one who chooses this medical option is fraught with worry, anxiety, loss, guilt, and concern. The potential for underlying psychological problems escalating during such procedures is high, as, for example, in cases of sexual abuse and rape, which can trigger anxieties and fears related to unresolved feelings of being assaulted and vulnerable. The psychoanalytic literature on this topic has so far examined and explored the treatment of infertility, focusing on traditional as well as more contemporary psychoanalytic explanations to understand and work with patients. Nevertheless, scant attention as been paid to the ongoing psychological world of women who undergo this procedure and the impact that their decisions have on their parenting. This chapter is offered as an attempt to understand this trajectory in a woman's emotional development and development as a mother.

Ms J and Ms M provide two examples of women who chose assisted reproductive technology to address their desire to have a child. The socio-political and medical climate that served as the backdrop for each woman varied considerably, as did their explorations and eventual understanding of the complexity of their decision and its eventual impact on their lives. Separated by a span of more than forty years, these two cases reveal that while the medical underpinnings (for the most part barring technological advances) of one's choice may have been similar, the emotional underpinnings contextualised by widely varying familial, cultural, and societal mores were marked by similarities and differences.

The reproductive histories or "reproductive story" for both Ms J and Ms M was kept hidden and out of our analytic inquiry for several years. Instead, their painstaking explorations of their current emotional difficulties revealed a complex history of early losses, which left both individuals with stunted emotional and sexual development. For Ms M, her adult narrative being shaped during the 1930s and 1940s, gave evidence of limited choice, a culture of silence (complicated by her history of immigration and other losses), and an utter absence in the medical and social structure to provide the necessary scaffolding for the difficult decisions she had to make. Furthermore, these silences and omissions resonated with Ms M's personal history of loss and its significant impact on her life. Compelled to become mute at the tender age of three, Ms M bore her "shame and sorrow" in private. Years of silence coloured by barely contained despair and rage rendered her helpless in the face of crucial choices. It was only towards the end of our work that Ms M could come to terms with the implications of her decision as she gradually gave voice to her innermost feelings. She could not reveal her decision to use donor sperm to conceive her children to anyone, though the lives of her children were undoubtedly coloured by it. My discomfort in bearing this secret (which I understood to be an extension of her guilt and shame) and my conveying this to her did not change her mind. This secret was borne in shame by herself and her husband and wielded its way like a knife into their ongoing relationship. However, in revealing it to me, I would now bear silent witness to her personal tragedy.

Almost sixty years after Ms M, Ms J conceived her child. Her son was a product of medical technology that had far surpassed what was available to Ms M. Yet, the procedure was no less complicated. Several unsuccessful attempts left Ms M depleted of emotional and physical strength. Guided only by her strong desire to have a child, and having the financial resources to engage in several procedures, Ms J had the luxury of using the best of medical technology that was available. But like Ms M, Ms J could not explore the complex feelings and fantasies surrounding her numerous "Petri dish" pregnancies and subsequent losses. Instead, her intrapsychic world was dominated by a compelling history of early trauma and loss, one that shaped Ms J's adult decisions and life trajectory. Her "reproductive history" (Jaffe & Diamond, 2005) could not emerge until much later, nor did she, like Ms M, seek any counselling during her numerous losses and experimental procedures.

For both Ms J and Ms M, their decision to use assisted reproductive technology, whether by necessity or by design, led to a complicated and affectively constricted portrayal of motherhood. Ms M disappointment, shame, and rage rendered her mute and helpless with her daughter, whom she could not control or manage. Unable to enlist the help of her husband, who was not biologically responsible for her "misfortune", as she put it, Ms M shouldered her burden in silence, victimised by the daughter who had no knowledge of her biological conception. For Ms J, she showered her son with love, becoming overly protective of his time and mind. While her fear that she could lose him was grounded in early losses and ruptured mother–child identifications, it nevertheless betrayed her despair that she only had one child and could never hope to have another. Motherhood for her had become the guillotine from which she could not escape.

For both Ms J and Ms M, their personal histories of trauma (coloured by themes of abandonment, shame, neglect, and guilt) became central to the work of therapy. However, it was in the explorations of their personal complex dynamics of motherhood and the use of assisted reproductive technology in the conception of their children that their personal narratives of trauma and infertility became more palpable and finally integrated and assimilated into a sense of self. Neither Ms J nor Ms M had sought any form of psychological treatment during the process of undergoing medical treatment. It was only several years later (for Ms M almost fifty years later, and for Ms J twelve years later) that we could begin to explore the profound impact of their life-changing decisions.

The implications for psychoanalytic involvement with this population are profound. Given the fact that many women who conceive a child using assisted reproductive technology do not seek psychoanalytic treatment during the time of conception, it would behoove us to keep in mind that such narratives may often appear later and during critical and challenging developmental phases in their lives. For Ms J, her narrative became more inclusive of her realities as her son entered his adolescent years. While it certainly resonated with her adolescence-related traumas, it also offered an entry into the exploration of his conception, her fears and anxieties, and her overwhelming feeling of loss. For Ms M, it was towards the end of our ongoing work (and her own life trajectory) that she revealed the secret behind her pregnancies. I have often wondered why she did not inform me earlier. While I can never know for sure, I believe that Ms M was determined to carry it to her grave (her husband was ailing and his demise was imminent). Yet, she needed someone to know, someone who could bear witness to her enormous struggle to bear her child, against all odds, and against prevailing social norms of conception and motherhood. Ms M was, one could say, the "outlier", yet she longed to belong, a feeling that was reminiscent of her early childhood years and one that had never quite left her.

Ms M and Ms J provide us hope into the indomitable human spirit that struggles to sustain life. I believe that in helping them tell their stories, their histories of trauma and infertility, and their dependency on assisted medical technology, that they finally found some emotional resolution.

References

Allison, G. H. (1997). Motherhood, motherliness, and psychogenic infertility. *Psychoanalytic Quarterly, 66*: 1–17.

Apfel, R. J., & Keylor, R. G. (2002). Psychoanalysis and infertility: myths and realities. *International Journal of Psycho-Analysis, 83*: 85–104.

Balsam, R. H. (1996). The pregnant mother and the body image of the daughter. *Journal of the American Psychoanalytical Assocation, 44*: 401–427.

Benedek, T. (1959). Parenthood as a developmental phase. *Journal of the American Psychoanalytical Association, 7*: 389–417.

Bibring, G. (1959). Some consideration of the psychological processes in pregnancy. *Psychoanalytic Study of the Child, 14*: 113–121.

Chodorow, N. J. (1978). *The Reproduction of Mothering*. Berkeley: University of California Press, revised edn. 1999.

Chodorow, N. J. (2003). "Too late": ambivalence about motherhood, choice, and time. *Journal of the American Psychoanalytic Association, 51*: 1181–1198.

Christie, G. L. (1997). The management of grief with infertile couples. *Journal of Assisted Reproduction Genetics, 14*: 189–191.

Downey, J. (1991). The new reproductive technologies: psychological issues for female patients. Paper presented at the 35th Winter Meeting of the American Academy of Psychoanalysis, New York, 5 December.

Gentile, K. (2013). Paper presented at meeting of the Association for the Psychoanalysis of Culture and Society, New Brunswick, NJ.

Jaffe, J., & Diamond, M. (2005). *Reproductive Trauma: Psychotherapy with Infertility and Pregnancy Loss Clients*. Washington, DC: American Psychological Association.

Kemeter, P., & Fiegel, J. (1998). Adjusting to life when assisted conception fails. *Human Reproduction, 13*: 1099–1105.

Leon, I. G. (1996). Reproductive loss: barriers to psychoanalytic treatment. *Journal of the American Academy of Psychoanalysis, 24*: 341–352.

Leon, I. G. (2010). Understanding and treating infertility: psychoanalytic considerations. *The Journal of the American Academy of Psychoanalysis and Dynamic Psychiatry, 38*: 47–75.

Rosen, A., & Rosen, J. (2005). *Frozen Dreams: Psychodynamic Dimensions of Infertility and Assisted Reproduction*. Hillsdale, NJ: The Analytic Press.

Vartiainen, H., Saarikoski, S., Halonen, P., & Rimon, R. (1994). Psychosocial factors, female fertility and pregnancy: a prospective study—Part I: fertility. *Journal of Psychosomatics and Gynaecology, 15*: 67–75.

PART II

CONCLUSION

CHAPTER SIX

Assisted reproduction as explored in *The Kids Are All Right*

Katherine MacVicar

The Kids Are All Right is a well-received film that deals in a comedic way with many of the difficulties faced by families that have conceived children through assisted reproduction. In this case, the parents are lesbian and the children have been conceived by artificial insemination, each woman in the couple having used the same donor so that the children are half-siblings. The pregnancies have been routine; the children are not regarded as fragile or as miracle children, but everyone is aware of the special status of having two mothers and no father. The children, two attractive teenagers, refer to their parents as "the two mums". There is a feeling in the film that the family is on display, and that the audience and the world are watching to see how the children fare. The mothers are eager to prove themselves, and do encourage the children to perform well, but it is moderated by the obvious loving commitment they have to them. The children have been informed, presumably in much earlier childhood, about the fact of a father, but have never met him. The audience is not told about male relatives or friends in the children's lives, but we presume that in this intelligent and sophisticated family, there have been some. What is portrayed is a normal caring family, but one that lacks a biological father. It is also one in which the parental couple has a sexuality that is given prominence in the film but that has complicated meanings to the children.

In the first scene, two boys ride their bikes in a very forceful way down the street, intent on speed and fun, yelling and whooping as they go. They are the son of the family and his friend. The camera looks up at them as they careen along. Motion and the outside world are everything. It is a scene of young masculinity bursting forth, and it is a harbinger of what is in store in the film, for among other themes the narrative highlights a young man's dilemma, a young man who has no father but two mothers. This episode is in contrast with a slightly later scene at home in the evening, in which the two mothers and the children are seated and the talk is of household chores and homework, of the interior and the sedate. It is a matter of emphasis and of the contrast between the primarily masculine and the primarily feminine. We also see their daughter's interactions with her friends; quietly and conversationally, they talk and joke about their lives and their futures but there is no physical action at all.

From the mothers' points of view, they want their parenting to be as good or better than that in heterosexual families. They are aware of being watched by friends, teachers, and the audience. Their late adolescent daughter, Joni, readying herself to go off to college, has the feeling that she has to try to be a perfect child. She attributes this to her family, but it also seems to be a basic part of the personality of this talented and thoughtful young woman. She is high-functioning, controlled, and serious. The situation is more fraught with their sixteen-year-old son, Laser. Even his name seems loaded with masculine associations. He is a star athlete at school and seems to be doing well, but the audience follows him as he watches his friend Clay roughhouse with his father and we see his intent gaze. We observe the sheer physicality of the father–son relationship, quite different from what occurs with his two mothers. Laser is fascinated with the rugged forcefulness of male relationships. He is struggling with masculine identifications and his longings for a masculine figure but also doesn't want to hurt the mothers' feelings.

During the summer before Joni will be leaving for college, he asks her if she will help him try to find their biological father, as she is now eighteen and able to access records from the sperm bank. She does so, and with trepidation they meet Paul, an attractive single man who has been quite reluctant to make any commitment to a relationship. Women pursue him and flock around him. There is an early scene showing

Paul in all his male glory, charming to women, and yet also the giver of nourishment because, as the owner of a restaurant, he feeds his customers wonderful healthy food. He seems an ideal father and mother combined. He also has an endless flow of words as he manages to make the children feel at home and enables them to overcome their initial discomfort. The children are very drawn in by his warmth and effusiveness, and he himself is very impressed with seeing his appealing children. He quickly falls in love with them without much thought about where this could lead. For the three of them, it seems at this point to be the answer to a longing they were scarcely aware of but that was there all along as an unconscious fantasy. There is a heady magic to it, as though each has found a love object that had been in their minds from the beginning. To the children, he is the father who can make everything possible, and to Paul they are wonderful beings that come from him and are his. Their rapid idealisation of him, however, seems based not on his being paternal towards them but much more on his being simply enchanted by them. None of them is a fully rounded human being to the other and we wonder, while enjoying the excitement of it all, when reality will hit.

With the imminent leaving of Joni for college, the film draws us into the two adolescents' situation of increasing emancipation and increasing readiness to leave home. The question arises as to what they will take away from the family in their own internal worlds when they leave, especially whether they will be "all right" and will be able to carry on. This is the prime matter suggested by the title and one that becomes more urgent as they approach independence. It is also raised as an issue because the parents are lesbian and so it is a somewhat unusual home. It is essential for adequate independent functioning and a feeling of being all right in the world that a young person has enough belief in the goodness of his objects and himself that he can deal with the anxieties and difficult external and internal situations that he will undoubtedly encounter. These internal images of good, helpful parents that have been identified with can be consulted, so to speak, to provide strength, support, and guidance (Bronstein, 2002). And part of being good is being normal. For Laser, the concern is that, despite the goodness of his parents, he is not quite normal because the parent who is most like him biologically did not play a part in his life so far. The relative unusualness of his family configuration raises for him new questions about his own goodness, adequacy, and masculinity.

The fact of an actual father, different from the internal picture of a paternal figure built up from interactions with the existing parents or with various male role models over the years, has become a much more important issue for him. This strong curiosity about the reality of an actual object is the same as the situation of the adopted child. Even though he may well have built up quite adequate internal pictures and ideas about his interactions with his parents that will be the bedrock of all future relationships, the adolescent, with his new appreciation of action in the world, wants to compare the notions he has built up with the so-called real things. Both children, but particularly Laser, have strong hopes of having a good relationship with a loving father who can provide something they felt was missing. Adolescents also sort out who they are by trying to sort out whom they are with. The easy-going, warm, fluent, and charming Paul is quite compelling to them as they compare him to themselves and to their parents. They see him at home in the bustling business he has created, the centre of attention. He seems the epitome of self-confident adulthood and fully sexual manhood.

The children are uncomfortable that their lesbian parents, Nic and Jules, do not know they have met Paul. They sense it will cause anxiety. Central to the film is that the parents' homosexuality is portrayed as one of the variations of normality (Meltzer, 1990). Yet its relative unusualness still seems to hover as a potential threat to the wellbeing of the children. In fact, it does seem to be a normal caring family, with each parent playing the role that best suits her character. The basic situation of unconscious bisexuality in everyone is well illustrated in the composition of the parents' relationship and parenting style. We have been introduced to the parents early in the film. Nic, intelligent, organised, and competent, is the breadwinner, the one who makes sure the children are fulfilling their obligations and who is much more strict. She takes the paternal role in the household. When she comes in, tired from work, she quickly sets out to make sure everything is in order and to communicate her own work ethic to the others. She sets rules and makes sure that responsibilities are fulfilled, and she confronts the children in a direct way about what she expects. She limits the children and embodies superego functions. She is the protector of the family both economically and morally. She protects Jules from the children; they respect her rules and Jules does not have to be the disciplinarian, a task for which she is not well suited. She also protects the children from Jules, who might well hold on to them longer than necessary out of her own insecurity. She tries to instill her own work ethic into Jules too, and the latter's more free-spirited and free-floating way of being bothers her.

Jules, a more scattered but basically warm person, is more conventionally motherly and nurturing. At this point, she is at home taking care of the needs of the children and seems quite content to continue to do so. She is still at sea concerning what she wants to do now that the children are so far along in adolescence and this has led to a tense and irritable atmosphere between the parents. Joni has graduated from high school and time is passing. Nic seems anxious and controlling. Jules' more urgent but somehow tenuous career plans seem to vacillate day by day as she procrastinates, apparently living in a cloud. By being a stay-at-home mother, she has put off taking hold of her life and her own development. She is a free-spirited character and resists choosing a profession and doing the hard work to get it started. Nic is frustrated and resentful that she is the only breadwinner and that the financial responsibility rests on her. She tries to mask her anger by drinking too much. The atmosphere is tense and overly nice.

In a scene that stirs up even more the already uncomfortable situation, we learn some of the details of their sexual life that, like their life together in general, is rather tense at the moment. We learn that they use male homosexual movies to stimulate sexual excitement, and we learn this because the tape briefly becomes very loud. We can also deduce that their sexual life has suffered from the resentment and anxieties of their other conflicts. The children momentarily overhear the tape, which makes the parents very uncomfortable, and the audience also feels the discomfort and the curiosity. Curiosity and strong feelings about parents' sexual life is not at all unique to children of assisted reproduction, but in those children it is given the additional valence of their fantasies and worries about how they were made. To young children, the role of the father in conception is often confusing, and despite being adolescent and knowing intellectually how things happen, this confusion can persist. And the fact of the parents being a homosexual couple also affects the fantasies that children have about the relationship. Especially for Laser, it seems bewildering and confusing. He must wonder about the role of a man and his penis in the world of intimacy and why his parents have seemingly rejected men.

Later the next day, Laser's friend Clay goes into the mothers' bedroom and starts the film so that Laser sees a segment of it. Joni has already apparently shrugged off the episode of hearing the tape; she seems more resilient, not yet much taken up into the sexual sphere, and also much more centred on getting ready to leave. But Laser is shaken, and in the midst of a disturbing but comedic conversation, we learn that the son and the two mothers are talking past each other when it comes to sexuality. The two women talk to him about the film and when he explains what happened, they observe correctly that he is troubled about it. His question is why their DVD viewing has taken the turn that it has (the audience is also presumably curious about this), and they assume he is hinting that he is gay. He then assumes they have somehow found out about Paul and so it all comes out that the biological father is now in the lives of the children. In this sequence, there has been the rapid introduction of several kinds of maleness rather different from the everyday fatherly attitude of Nic: Paul, the carefree heterosexual father, the homosexual couple on the DVD, and the delinquent teenage friend, with the confused boy himself watching everything, very concerned about what fits him and very much wanting to find something good. The pain of his search for whom he comes from, and therefore who he is himself, becomes palpable.

The filmmaker also wants the audience to feel stirred up and uncomfortable about the parental sexuality. We become Laser, with a host of worries and questions. Seeing the pornographic film is a limited but unfortunate lapse of privacy that is upsetting for Laser, who is concerned about his own sexuality, especially whether or not he can feel he is a good person. The film makes it harder and the parent's homosexuality also make it harder. Jules realises that he is upset and does explain to him that lesbian pornographic films use straight actresses with ideal bodies, that they are largely made for male audiences, and that male homosexual films seem more real, but one feels he is still quite confused about both the parents and the film. He cannot really make sense of it. And it feels quite painful that the parents assume that he is gay and is experimenting homosexually. They are all out of touch with each other, though it is also important to point out that all parents experience this from time to time with their rapidly changing adolescents. It's moderated by their sincere concern for him and the real wish to help him make sense of things, though they themselves are uncomfortable. However, Jules' explanation does not really make sense. The women themselves are only dimly aware of what the film means to them, but Jules makes a heartfelt attempt, and it is certainly better than nothing.

Jules' willingness to be truthful is touching as far as it goes; she has grasped a part of his dilemma and knows she has to be frank about it. This seems to be a moment of real contact in which her intent to help is more important than what she says; she realises that he has an important question, that it is not frivolous. The interaction has been uncomfortable and strange, but at the end the pressure has been reduced to a degree. Jules is a person who can come through when she needs to, and she gives him enough information to be somewhat reassuring but not so much as to drag him further into their personal lives. Most parents can resonate with such moments. But there are many unaddressed concerns. We are invited to think that pornographic films are just a normal part of intimate life and should not be brought up in any way. And Laser does not do so; he tries to be blasé about pornography in general but to ask about the specific type. For adolescents struggling to maintain a sense of goodness in their parents' sexual life, any pornography is likely to feel disturbing. It is not only a shock because it is gay male pornography, it is a shock because it is any kind of pornography. The parents' distress shows us that it's not only that they don't want to parade their sex lives in front of the children, but that they don't want the children to think that they are involved in something the latter, with their youthful idealism, could think of as degrading. And Laser is also left with confusion about the penis and the role it plays in the connections of intimacy.

In many ways, the most basic identifications that the young child makes to the parents are made to parents regarded as bisexual (Boswell, 2002). The child tends to regard each parent as containing the qualities, and often the actual body parts, of the other. Thus children have fantasies of the father with breasts, the mother with a penis inside, the mother's womb full of babies that she produces at will, and so on. But the child also has a relationship with the qualities of the parents that are symbolised by body parts, for instance the strength of the mother is seen as her having the father inside her, or the gentleness of the father is seen as his having taken in the the mother. Thus the basic qualities of each sex, regarded as conventionally masculine or feminine, can be gleaned from a parent of either sex. We have long known that it is quite possible for a woman to raise strong boys because of identifications with her own strength of character, persistence, and courage—qualities that are conventionally masculine but appear in both sexes. The same applies to the so-called feminine qualities of caring, sensitivity, and devotion. In a same-sex couple, it is the same; each person has a different blend of qualities that contribute to the way she expresses her role as a parent. In this couple, Nic is the more protective paternal figure and Jules is the more nurturing and caring maternal one, not that the roles are split but that the emphasis is different in each character.

The children also have a relationship with their parents as a couple that has a special bond that excludes them, and identifications with that creative couple are very important to the child's own creativity. This relationship is sometimes seen by the child as ideally good, that is, the parents helping and nourishing each other. Particularly it is seen as the father using his strength and his penis to repair and feed the mother, who, the child fears, has been damaged by his own aggression. In this view, children are relieved that the mother has another to rely on for comfort and support, and they do not have to worry too much about doing her harm her since damage can potentially be repaired. On the other hand, a child whose relationship with the parents is not secure, either through his own heightened aggression or through family circumstances, can see the parent's private relationship as harmful or destructive, as the mother being further hurt by the father, as the mother extracting revenge on the father, or as an activity intended to damage or humiliate the child. This can also be expressed in the language of body parts, such as the fear that the father's penis is damaging, the mother's vagina is engulfing, and so on.

Laser's anxiety and curiosity seem to be a continuation of the child's earliest researches about what it is that parents do when they are alone together. Children have all sorts of sexual fantasies about the parents based on where they are developmentally, but basically these are both fantasies about a good, helpful relationship and a bad, destructive one. On the surface, we might think that Laser's concerns are about the part the penis plays in the relationship, and that is probably a part of it, but I think on a deeper level, the concern is whether the parents are helping, consoling, and nourishing each other or whether they are hurting each other. The film of the hyper-masculine gay men is a symbol of something disruptive, something that is self-centred rather than loving. Laser has undoubtedly picked up on the issues that are brewing between the parents and is responding in an anxious way to their general state of discontent as well as to the sexual revelation. His dilemma is how to make sense of this and continue to believe in the goodness and rightness of his parents. The title of the film, I think, points to this;

the children can only be securely all right if they can feel the parents' relationship is predominantly good.

Children are aware from an early age that the parents have a bodily relationship. Perhaps this is even present from birth as an unconscious fantasy, primitive though it might be. And they have fantasies about all the erotogenic parts of the body and how they might be involved based on their developmental levels. And yet most children also prefer to deny that parents are sexual. It must be most confusing to Laser to know his parents don't have a penis (unless it is the hidden penis of the mother, a common early fantasy and one that may well be held on to throughout life) and yet are thinking about it and watching it. Some of the complexities of bisexuality and homosexuality have been pushed in front of him, and despite the reassurance that Jules gives him, he goes away with much unknown.

The following scene of the dinner to which Paul is invited to meet the parents is also quite uncomfortable for everyone except Paul, who seems at home anywhere. An event that occurred in the very private sphere, the conception of the children, is now being shared in a public light. Nic has many reservations about it, since she feels the integrity of the family is threatened, while the children are hoping that all three parents will like each other and that the meeting will be cordial. Laser seems to wish that Paul could be integrated into the couple somehow, bolstering his sense of normality.

Paul wants to know the family and has been moved by meeting the children. It has jarred him into questioning his uncommitted life. He wants to continue the relationship, and in his warm but rather impulsive way asks Jules if she would do some landscaping at his house since this is the type of business she thinks of starting. Jules, who is rather at a loose end at the moment, agrees. This is over the objections of Nic, who senses the possible complications. Although she is portrayed as formal, insecure, and somewhat rigid, she is also the realistic and protective one who knows danger may be on the horizon and who wants to prevent it. She senses the competitive issues between the adults, such as whether the children have been stolen from Paul. Whose children are they really? Are they rightfully his? Can they be stolen back? She feels the danger of Paul inserting himself into the family, the very thing the children think they want.

At this point, Paul is an idealised figure to the children, a wonderful father who has found them at last. This is not a state that can last, since

Paul has also been absent all of their lives and must also be seen as a rejecting, hateful figure, someone who has not shown the slightest interest in them. These fantasies that are such polar opposites are one of the things that make it so difficult for children to meet their birth parents. The children have not had the opportunity to test the reality of a father against their infantile fantasies about him, and he has never moderated into a mixed figure, someone who can be both liked for some qualities and disliked for others. Instead, there are wildly disparate points of view about him and they can change quickly.

The relationship between Jules and Paul proceeds rapidly, and as they plan the garden they also find themselves having much in common. Now that he's employing Jules, Paul also has more contact with Laser. In a very moving scene, the latter asks Paul why he became a sperm donor. Paul begins in a joking way but sees that Laser is hurt by this, so he ends up saying he wanted to help people have the babies they so much wanted and that he's very glad he did it. It's palpable how much Laser wants to feel that something serious went into his making, that it's not just something Paul did lightly, as a way to make money. He desperately wants to see himself as coming out of something normal and good, not something abnormal or out of kilter. It is one of the most touching moments in the film that Paul grasps this and responds in an understanding way. It also puts Paul in a much more paternal light. Paul has also noticed the behaviour of Clay, the semi-delinquent and risk-taking friend of Laser, and he tells Laser that this friend is not good for him. So now there is also Paul, in addition to the parents, warning Laser against Clay. All three adults are subliminally worried that delinquency is a danger for Laser as he struggles with both good and bad identifications. Initially, Laser is angry that Paul acts as a father rather than a buddy. But he seems to watch Clay more.

A few scenes later, we see the end of the friendship with Clay when Laser observes him tormenting a dog. Laser objects to the behaviour but Clay continues. They struggle and Laser manages to release the dog, which Clay had started to beat with his belt. Disgusted by the cruelty that he now saw so clearly in his friend's delinquent behaviour, a cruelty that seems to escalate as the film goes on, he walks away. Clay no longer seems appealing; this is not the kind of young man he wants to be. The audience is relieved as it sees him decisively turning away from something bad, and rejecting this cruel representation of masculinity.

Very quickly, Jules' uncertainties about her own life and Paul's general impulsiveness have led them into starting an affair, something they do without much thought. The audience immediately feels this is a transgression that is serious and destructive, and that things have started to spin out of control. We see Jules starting to feel this when she angrily fires her helper who realises what is going on. Paul has broken into the parental couple, and it quickly escalates into the fantasy that he can be the father of this family. It is not just Laser who is trying to sort out the kind of man he will be; Paul also undergoes wide swings in his ideas about manhood. He gives up his non-serious girlfriend, continuing to have more contact with the children and intensifying the affair with Jules. But he also takes Joni on his motorcycle, something Nic had explicitly forbidden. He seems to want to be the kind of father figure who overturns the rules, who sets up a new world order. It would be one more oriented to the outside, looser, more in the moment. It is a challenge to Nic, and at this moment it seems to be winning, at least with the children, who are still enchanted. Nic, not yet knowing about the affair but sensing something in the atmosphere, feels her fears of the family's unravelling are coming true. During dinner with friends, she becomes very upset while talking about her family life, and leaves abruptly.

Joni, perhaps subliminally aware of the family rupture, finally shows that she is quite anxious about leaving home and the advent of her own sexuality. At her graduation party, she drinks too much and tries to seduce a platonic friend. Up until this moment, she seems to have been avoiding contact with her sexual feelings, remaining in the role of a good asexual girl. She has not appeared to show interest in either sex. Paul's arrival, with his sexual ease and charm, together with her imminent departure, has stirred her towards sexual interests that seem to come upon her suddenly. Paul is now taking a greater and greater role with Jules and the children both. Nic, still unaware of the betrayal, has become the beleaguered one, trying to limit all these rather overexcited relationships. She agrees to go over to dinner at Paul's house with the family, a dinner that seems to be Paul's way of saying that he by now almost belongs in the family. She is not quite sure if she can handle the situation, and she is determined not to drink but to face the situation with a clear head. It is dawning on her that something quite momentous is required of her to hold the family together, to protect it from dissolution, and that she has to have the strength to keep Paul at his proper distance in the affections of Jules and the children.

During the dinner, Nic and Paul do discover points in common and the atmosphere is more comfortable. The women share how they first met. Jules went into the emergency room where Nic was working during her training. Jules was anxious, had begun to breathe too quickly, and became panicky over the feeling that she was suffocating. Nic administered the time-honoured treatment of breathing into a paper bag, and so began a relationship that seemed based on Nic taking care of and rescuing Jules. These confessions lead to Paul revealing that he had not been much of a student, and the general atmosphere becomes one of the adults letting their hair down and sharing more of their preferences and weaknesses. But during the unburdening, Nic goes into the bathroom and discovers Jules' hair in Paul's shower.

At the crisis point, Nic confronts Jules, who does not try very hard to deny the affair. Jules seems to realise fairly quickly that the interlude was a kind of magical fantasy and immediately is regretful. Her feelings, always right on the surface, are distress for the pain she has caused, regret, and the desire to make amends. For Jules, the affair seems to have been a kind of dream or a fling, something that could provide some relief from the challenges of putting together a career, but Paul is entertaining fantasies of taking Jules and Laser away from Nic and starting a new family. He has been drawn in to the fantasy of the children that an actual male figure will create a better family. Jules rebuffs him, horrified by the misstep she has made. The children also are horrified at the way things have spiralled out of control and quickly back away from Paul, the wolf in sheep's clothing. He immediately becomes a very bad figure to them, and topples from his place of ideal father. There is a period of estrangement between the two women, but when the children ask anxiously whether they are going to get a divorce, Jules speaks sincerely about how complicated adults' feelings are, how easy it is to make a mistake that you regret, and how much work a marriage is. The women reconcile and when Paul comes around again just before Joni is to leave for college, the children will not talk to him, and Nic sends him away with the words, "Get your own family".

The family takes Joni off to college with the repair of the parental couple still very recent, and we see her momentary panic when she thinks the family has just left after dropping her off at her dormitory. Although in general she's quite an independent young woman, she too has been shaken by what has happened and needs to feel reassured that she is loved and cared about. Ending on a note of family solidarity, the now-reconstituted couple leave Joni at school and prepare for life as a threesome.

As the parents and Laser drive back from installing Joni in college, Laser remarks that he is very glad they aren't getting a divorce because they are too old to do that. This is said in a cheerful tone, as though he is relieved and happy. He doesn't have to worry that his experiment with a father has ruined things and his calling them old (they are in their forties) seems to indicate an acceptance of how things are, that they are in the parental generation and he can still depend on them. He seems to have achieved an acceptance about his lack of a father and to feel content and grateful for what he does have, two imperfect but very committed parents.

The story is an elaboration of many important psychological themes in the lives of children of assisted reproduction. Whenever there is a biological parent whom the child has never met, there is bound to be curiosity, particularly as the child gets older. There are fantasies about that parent, both good and bad. Information given to younger children about where they come from and the presence of a biological parent different from the caretaking parent often seems to have no effect at first, though in an insecure child it may stir up anxieties. Usually, the information goes underground. But it also tends to activate and give a certain reality to the "family romance" fantasy, that one has a different, usually better, family somewhere out there. The child, of course, has no chance to compare these fantasies with the reality of an actual person. Perhaps the child feels he comes from royalty or people of high standing, and that he was somehow lost, stolen from them, or separated by some disaster. On the other hand, there are also fantasies about the absent parent as a monstrously bad person, malevolently abandoning the baby. But it sets up the wish to find the parent again, and during the emancipatory years of adolescence when curiosity about the world of objects in general is so much in the forefront, it can become quite strong. Here, we see played out first the fantasy, strikingly held by Laser, that Paul is ideal, that he can provide a role model that will dramatically improve everything. And certainly during the first few meetings, the atmosphere is one of excitement and great possibility.

Nic does not share in this, though Jules does, to a degree. Nic seems to realise that forces have been released, and is fearful of Paul's effect on the family. It is her position as the protector of the family that is being threatened; yet she tries to see beyond herself and to bear the uncomfortable situation. She also realises the normality of the children's wish to know their father and she tries to be rational about it, hoping that by supervising the contact she can prevent the untoward from happening. She very much wants the kids to come out of this "all right", both because of her concern for them and her wish to prove herself as a parental figure. Jules does not seem as thoughtful about Paul's potential effect on the children; she seems to live much more in the present and to participate in their happiness and excitement. There is quite a difference of character between the two women, with Nic coolly looking ahead and planning for eventualities and Jules ruled by the moment. Planning is not Jules' strong suit and it renders her more susceptible to her immediate feelings.

During the film, we see the unspooling of the children's fantasy that Paul will be a magical rescuer. By the end, Paul has become much more than a hypothetical threat; he is an agent of destruction and must be sent away entirely for the safety of the family. Now that their biological father is actually present, we see how hard it is for the adolescents to judge him realistically; he is either idealised or seen as terribly destructive and threatening figure. Adopted children or children born of ART share this task of having to face the difficulty of seeing this parent in a realistic light. The resolution in the film comes when the family bands together to expel the intruder, firmly making him the "bad" one, whereas realistically they all participated in the situation. The expulsion may seem harsh, but Paul is blamed for trying to destroy the couple, and one of the themes of the film is that the parental couple is important, whether same-sex or opposite-sex, and it is terribly important to the children as they go off to live their own lives and form their own families. The couple has created and formed them and it is this creativity with which they will identify in their own lives. Both children respond with anxiety that they have precipitated the disruption of the parental bond. It seems that responsibility for this situation has to be firmly fixed outside the family such that the children can continue their development without feeling they have destroyed their parents.

With adequate parenting, children don't usually develop sustained curiosity about a biological parent until later in development. Given their very different sense of time and the immediacy of their needs, information about something that happened before they were born doesn't really become important until they are much more mature cognitively and are ready to struggle with their own independence and their real origins as a person. Before that, their windows onto the world are the day-to-day parents who are there satisfying their real needs. And their sexual theories and their thoughts about where babies come from are always taken from their own development, despite whatever information they have been given, until their cognitive development allows them to arrive at a more correct picture. They tend to hear information about assisted conception in terms of their own theories and the fantasies appropriate to their own level of development. In adolescence, with its strong object hunger, the facts of what really happened do become important and the need to sort out the real events becomes stronger. Laser wants to compare his fantasies of a father about whom he's been told with who he actually is. At depth, though, he retains the old fantasies and the wish for a very special father, a father without limits, a king perhaps, or a hero. How can you reconcile that picture with someone who would break up his family, the source of his stability? I think his wishful fantasy of a special, heroic, wonderful father comes crashing down to earth. The bubble bursts. His psychological father, derived from both parents but largely centred on Nic, is what he, at base, relies on.

Also touched upon in the film is the child's exclusion from and interest in the parents' intimate life, and the many feelings that surround this. Joni seems to accept the parents' relationship and its homosexuality quite comfortably at first. She does not seem to be concerned about her sexual orientation. She does not worry about femininity. When her friends tease her about sex and boys, she seems above it. She does not react much to overhearing a bit of the sex tape. She seems to be comfortable with having her own life at college and comfortable with her own relative lack of sexuality. We do not see her anxiety until her senior graduation party, when out of worry about how she'll manage away from home, she is very seductive with a boy who had been a platonic friend. But this all seems rather normal and what is conveyed is that she is pretty clear about who she is as a person and that the anxieties she does have are under control. She knows what kind of young woman she is. And you don't get the feeling that she has been as swept up with Paul or as reactive to him as has her brother. Like her mother Nic, she is more self-contained. She has her fears and resentments, but you sense she will get through them with only the usual difficulties.

With Laser, a couple of years younger, it's more fraught and one sees him (via Clay) try to intrude and get into the mysterious and rather upsetting secrets of the parental sexual relationship. He's trying to find himself and his own masculinity in many of his objects; Nic's strength and productivity, his friend Clay's hyper-masculine recklessness, and Paul's carefree lifestyle. Regarding Clay, Laser has been rather a follower of this boy and has been watching and going along with behaviours that seem dangerous and exaggerated. He is a "bad self" sort of character; the destructive behaviours are located in him and Laser is a watcher. For example, it is he who is interested in the parent's sexual life, not Laser, at least overtly. A turning point for Laser comes when he sees Clay being cruel to a dog. He rejects him, turning away from recklessness as he realises the cruelty that the friend really expresses.

After he witnesses the effects of their affair, he also rejects Paul, not even looking at him through the window when he comes to say goodbye to Joni. Initially, he wished that Paul would become a part of the family, but with the affair he must suddenly face that these wishes have had a destructive outcome. He sees that Paul, while not cruel, is thoughtless and impulsive. Paul's wishes to take over the family seem self-centred and childish, more like a fantasy than something taken seriously. Laser quickly turns away. I think it shows us that Laser's internal image of a good psychological father, largely derived from the strong and productive qualities of Nic, has been disrupted but not destroyed by the stresses of their marriage, and that his need to have his family intact and good supercedes everything else (Britton, 1996).

Discussion

I think that augmented and often rather sudden states of disillusionment and mourning distinguish children who are the products of ART from their peers who are not dealing with the fantasies about an absent biological parent. While children whose parents are around most of the time can gradually get used to their virtues as well as their faults and deficits, the meetings with biological parents tend to be compressed and infrequent. They are almost always disappointing and painful, necessitating the mourning for lost dreams. The probability that this is so sudden and final can be unbearably painful. Children with parents who are present have years to face that they are far from omnipotent, while children of ART may very precipitously lose this hope. In the film, the children rebound rather quickly, but this is not always the case. Although it is painful, it is undoubtedly an important milestone for the child of assisted reproduction to come to terms with this, and a good indicator of the young person's progress towards emancipation.

I think the film is psychologically correct when it shows us that it is not primarily the biological sex of the parents that determines children's overall health, as well as their sexual identification; it the role that each parent plays and their more general human qualities. It's important to have in the family someone who will set down rules and stick to them, and someone who will make clear and show in behaviour what is bad and what is good. We see in Laser's struggle with the qualities that Clay epitomises that parental intervention helps him turn away from destructive and aggressive behaviour towards something more constructive. Nic was in the forefront of his ability to identify with a more caring male role.

We also see the effects when the private life of parents erupts into the public sphere. While inevitable at times, it is destabilising and stirs up anxieties. The idea of parents of whatever sex having an inviolable private space in which they can give to each other what children cannot, and can have ways of helping each other with the inevitable strains of parenthood, is helpful to children as well as comforting. If parents can have a private life, then children can more comfortably emancipate and look forward to their own lives. In the case of the children in the film, it also means that one can get beyond being the special child who must do very well to show that he or she comes from a normal family and has turned out "all right". The parents here have weathered an emotional storm that is much more meaningful than conventional normality, and this can help the children get beyond the mere "good performance" aspects of much of their lives.

Conclusion

The film takes us into a family, all of whose members are trying to resolve normative crises. The children are adolescents, forming their sexual identities and getting ready to leave home, while the lesbian parents are experiencing their own conflicts over work and the impending loss of the children. The sudden advent of the children's biological father stirs up these conflicts to the breaking point, but they are able to be resolved due to the basic strengths of the parents and overall positive development of the children, aided by projecting into the biological father the role of the "bad one" and then rejecting him. One of the greatest psychological hazards of being a child of assisted reproduction is the proliferation of fantasies about the missing parent and the sudden collapse of the child's hopes for this relationship. Although it did not happen in the film, this can lead to extended states of mourning and feelings of badness that are hard to master.

References

Boswell, J. (2002). The Oedipus complex. In: C. Bronstein (Ed.), *Kleinian Theory: A Contemporary Perspective*. London and Philadelphia: Whurr.

Britton, R. (1996). The Oedipus situation and the depressive position. In: R. Anderson (Ed.), *Clinical Lectures on Klein and Bion*. London and New York: Routledge.

Bronstein, C. (2002). What are internal objects? In: C. Bronstein (Ed.), *Kleinian Theory: A Contemporary Perspective*. London and Philadelphia: Whurr.

Meltzer, D. (1996). The introjective basis of polymorphous tendencies in adult sexuality. In: *Sexual States of Mind*. Perthshire, Scotland: Clunie Press.

INDEX

117